GREAT DISHES FROM SPAIN

JANET MENDEL

PHOTOGRAPHY BY
JOHN JAMES WOOD

SANTANA BOOKS

GREAT DISHES FROM SPAIN
Published by Ediciones Santana S.L.
Apartado 41,
29650 Mijas Pueblo (Málaga), Spain
Tel: (0034) 952 485 838. Fax: (0034) 952 485 367
info@santanabooks.com

Text copyright©Janet Mendel
Photography copyright©John James Wood

Design: Chris Fajardo

No part of this book may be reproduced or
transmitted in any form or by any means without
the prior written permission of the publishers.

Printed in Spain by Gráficas San Pancracio S.L.

Depósito Legal: MA-13/2006
ISBN: 84-89954-48-8

Janet Mendel has been researching and writing about Spain's national and regional cuisine for nearly 40 years. In this successor to *Tapas*, from which some of the recipes are taken, she and acclaimed food photographer John James Wood collaborate to take an expanded look at the country's infinite variety of dishes. Mendel's other publications include the classic *Cooking in Spain*, first published by Santana in 1987, the award-winning *Traditional Spanish Cooking* and the highly praised *My Kitchen in Spain*. Wood produced food illustrations for multi-national corporations in the USA for some 20 years before basing himself in Spain where he now does landscape and location photography as well as studio work.

GREAT DISHES FROM SPAIN

CONTENTS

An Introduction to Spanish Cooking   **7**

1. THE *TAPAS* EXPERIENCE   **10**

Shellfish Cocktail, *Salpicón de Mariscos*
Mussels Vinaigrette, *Mejillones a la Vinagreta*
Marinated Fresh Anchovies, *Boquerones al Natural*
Roasted Pepper Salad, *Ensalada de Pimientos Asados*
Catalan Tomato Toasts, *Pan amb Tomat*
BEST HAM IN THE WORLD AND SOME VERY DISTINCTIVE SAUSAGE
Canary Islands Wrinkly Potatoes with Spicy Herb Sauces, *Papas Arrugadas con Mojo*
Green Chilli Sauce, *Mojo Verde*
Red Chilli Sauce, *Mojo Colorado*
Hot Potatoes, *Patatas Bravas*
Marinated Fried Fish, *Cazón en Adobo*
Prawns in Raincoats, *Gambas en Gabardinas*
SPAIN'S DELECTABLE CHEESES
Spanish Potato Omelette, *Tortilla Española*
Spicy Pork Kebabs, *Pinchitos Morunos*
Garlic-Sizzled Prawns, *Gambas al Ajillo*
SIPPING SPAIN - WHAT TO DRINK WITH *TAPAS*, WITH DINNER
Red Wine Fruit Punch, *Sangría*

2. STARTERS, SOUPS & SIDES   **46**

Orange and Cod Salad, *Remojón*
Galician Pork Pie, *Empanada Gallega*
GASTRONOMIC SOUVENIRS

CONTENTS

Eggs Scrambled With Mushrooms, Prawns and Green Garlic, *Huevos Revueltos Con Setas, Gambas y Ajetes*
Baked Eggs, Flamenco Style, *Huevos a la Flamenca*
Peppers Stuffed With Fish, *Pimientos de Piquillo Rellenos con Pescado*
Grilled Prawns With Romesco Sauce, *Langostinos a la Plancha con Salsa de Romesco*
Octopus, Galician Style, *Pulpo a la Gallega*
Clams, Fishermen's Style, *Almejas a la Marinera*
Cold Andalusian Tomato Soup, *Gazpacho Andaluz*
Cold White Garlic Soup With Grapes, *Ajo Blanco con Uvas*
ESSENTIAL FLAVOUR: OLIVE OIL
Seafood Chowder with Sherry, *Gazpachuelo*
Castilian Garlic Soup, *Sopa Castellana*
Garnished Broth, *Sopa de Picadillo*
Galician Soup, *Caldo Gallego*
Spinach With Raisins and Pine Nuts, *Espinacas con Pasas y Piñones*
Summer Vegetable Stew, *Pisto*
Broad Beans with Serrano Ham, *Habas con Jamón*
Spanish Potato Casserole, *Cazuela de Patatas "A Lo Pobre"*
Farm-Style Fried Bread Crumbs, *Migas a la Cortijera*

3. MAIN DISHES   90

Asturian Casserole of Beans and Sausages, *Fabada Asturiana*
Chickpeas with Spinach, *Garbanzos con Espinacas*
Lentil Pot, *Potaje de Lentejas*
Paella With Seafood, *Paella Con Mariscos*
THE SPICES OF LIFE
Pasta Paella with Seafood, *Fideuá*
Garlic Mayonnaise, *Alioli*
Basque-Style Hake, *Merluza a la Vasca*
Baked Fish with Potatoes, *Pescado al Horno*

GREAT DISHES FROM SPAIN

Bream, Grilled on its Back, *Besugo a la Espalda*
Chicken Sizzled with Garlic, *Pollo al Ajillo*
Chicken in Almond Sauce, *Pollo en Pepitoria*
Herb-Marinated Pork Loin, *Lomo en Adobo*
Lamb Braised With Sweet Peppers, *Cordero al Chilindrón*
Bull's Tail (Braised Ox-Tail), *Rabo de Toro*
Braised Partridge, Toledo Style, *Perdiz Estofada a la Toledana*

4. PASTRIES AND PUDDINGS — 124

Catalan Custard with Burnt Sugar Topping, *Crema Catalana*
Creamy Rice Pudding With Cinnamon, *Arroz Con Leche*
Santiago Almond Torte, *Torta de Santiago*
Sweet Fritters, *Buñuelos*
Anise-Flavoured Holiday Rings, *Roscos de Navidad*
Meringue Milk Ice, *Leche Merengada*
HOLIDAY SWEETS AND NATURAL DELIGHTS

Glossary — 140

Index — 142

An Introduction to Spanish Cooking

A flamenco flounce. The swish and click of a Spanish fan. Gold embroidery on a matador's suit of lights. The scent of jasmine in the night air. Golden rice in a *paella* pan. Prawns sizzling in garlicky olive oil. Spain is sensual, tactile, a rich and flavourful panorama of colour, sounds, aroma and touch. And so is the cuisine.

Spain's cooking is quintessentially Mediterranean — the bright and sunny flavours of olive oil, fresh fruits and vegetables, seafood and wine. But its styles and flavours vary considerably according to region, and it's a large country.

Compared to the cuisines of neighbouring France and Italy, Spanish food seems more exotic, due to the influence of the Moors (Muslims from Arabia and North Africa), who occupied Spain for many centuries, right up until 1492, when the last Moorish stronghold, the Kingdom of Granada, was defeated by the troops of King Ferdinand and Queen Isabella.

The Moorish heritage shows up in the use of ground almonds and spices such as saffron, cinnamon, nutmeg and sesame, even in savoury dishes; in the love of rice dishes such as *paella*, (the Arabs introduced rice-growing to Spain); and in the honeyed sweets and pastries. Even today, you will find similarities between Spanish food and the cuisine of nearby Morocco, just across the Straits of Gibraltar. But, also many differences.

Thus, Spanish cooking includes the wide use of pork, ham and sausage, which, of course, are forbidden in the Muslim diet. More importantly, after Columbus set sail from Spain and discovered a New World, Spain in the 15th and 16th centuries became a world power, exploring and colonising three continents. The Spanish *conquistadores* didn't just discover gold — they discovered new foods, such as tomatoes, potatoes and maize, chocolate, beans and squash, peppers, pineapple and avocados, which eventually enriched Spanish and European diets.

GREAT DISHES FROM SPAIN

Don't expect Spanish cooking to be like Mexican or Hispanic food. While the Hispanic countries of the Americas share some of the dishes from colonial Spain, Spain's own cooking is nothing at all like the indigenous Indian cooking of the Americas — no corn *tortillas*, no hot-hot chilli. No *"salsa."*

So, what's Spanish? Best-known dishes are: *paella*, saffron-rice with chicken and seafood, typical of the eastern regions of Spain where rice is grown; *gazpacho*, a cold soup of raw ingredients from Andalusia in southern Spain; *fabada,* a hearty bean and sausage casserole from Asturias in the north; *romesco*, a fabulous sauce of sweet peppers and crushed nuts, which the Catalans serve with grilled fish; *cocido*, a meal-in-a-pot, typical of the capital, Madrid, but, in fact, served in every region of the country, and *tortilla*, which in Spain is a thick, round potato omelette. Add to that list superb seafood dishes from all the coastal regions — Spain consumes more

INTRODUCTION

fish and shellfish than any other European country — plus an enticing array of sweets.

Spanish products appreciated abroad include: fine olives, particularly the Seville *manzanillas*; capers; oranges; avocados; saffron; dried figs and raisins; almonds and other nuts; cured *serrano* ham; canned shellfish.

You can create authentic Spanish food in your own kitchen, with ingredients easy to find in local shops. The selection of recipes in this book represents the best of Spain's cuisine, the regional "signature" dishes, some rustic, country-style, others with sophisticated flair. Check out the special sections for more information about Spanish wine, ham, cheeses, olive oil, spices, and sweets.

¡Que aproveche! Enjoy! Take advantage of Spain's great culinary heritage.

A note about the recipes:

For the convenience of cooks on several continents, measurements for ingredients are given in metric, British imperial measures, and American standard measures. The American measurements appear in parentheses. Also where American terminology differs from British, the American word is in parentheses, e.g. aubergine (eggplant).

1
the *tapas* experience

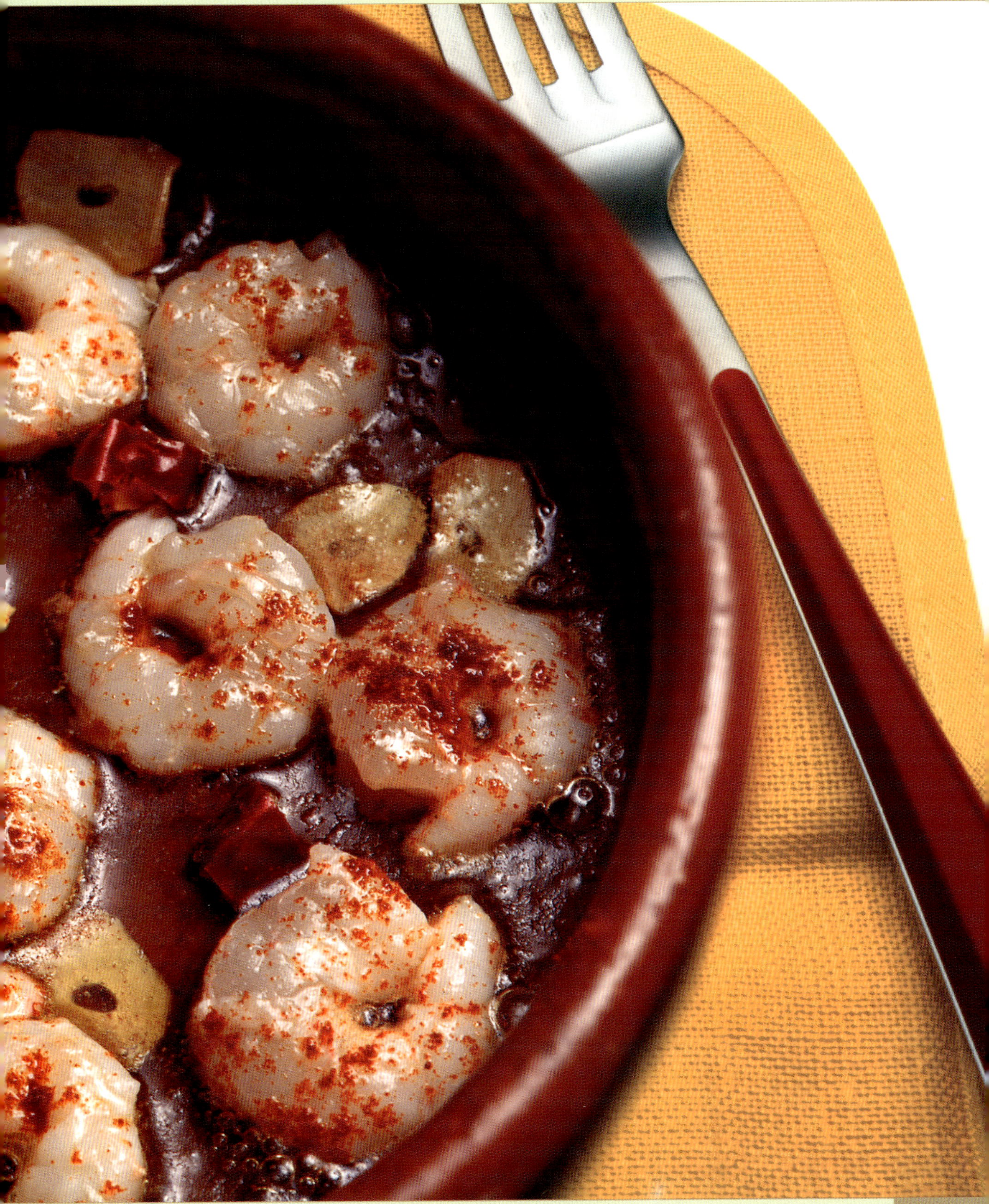

The *Tapas* Experience

Just follow the crowds through this doorway, into the cool interior of a typical *tasca* or wine bar. Multi-coloured tiles line the walls, while clay-tiled floors shine with the patina of years of footsteps. Barrels of wine are stacked behind the bar. From wooden beams hang whole hams and links of sausages, ropes of garlic and peppers.

You order a glass of wine and the barman asks if you would like a *tapa*. *Tapas* are small portions of foods, both hot and cold, served in wine bars to accompany a *copa* of *fino* (dry Spanish sherry), *vino* (wine), *cava* (sparkling wine), *sidra* (cider), or draught beer. You can enjoy *tapas* in most bars before the lunch hour (in Spain this is very late — *tapas* at 1pm, lunch at 2pm or after), and again before dinner (7 to 9pm, with dinner later yet). *Tapas* are a splendid introduction to the wide variety of Spanish cuisine because you can share a selection of them among several friends.

They are served in bars in every region of Spain, each of which has its variations on the theme. The word *tapa* means "cover". In winemaking regions, such as Jerez, home of sherry, a tiny saucer was customarily placed to cover a glass of wine in order to keep the little fruit flies from swarming in. A tidbit of food placed on the dish helped attract clients to the wine bar, so the cook — usually the owner's wife — would out-do herself to make more and better ones. In some bars this snack is served free with the wine.

Tapa-hopping is part of the convivial Spanish way of life. With a few friends you stop in at several bars to have a glass of wine and sample the *tapa* specialities of each. It's customary to stand up at the bar, but sometimes you sit at a table and order *raciones*, whole rations or plates of food to share. In northern Spain, *tapas* are called *pinchos* or *pintxos*, bits of food skewered on a toothpick. These might include a quail's egg with gherkin and cocktail onion, a cherry tomato plus chunk of tuna and olive, or a meatball, or green pepper and anchovy.

Here's a tantalising taste of some of the dishes — hot and cold — that you might find in a *tapa* bar.

Certainly there'll be the superb ham, both *serrano*, or mountain-cured, and the pricey *jamón ibérico*, produced from a special breed of pigs which feed on acorns. This salt-cured ham is served raw, very thinly sliced. Pair it with *fino* sherry for a truly marvellous taste sensation.

And, of course, olives. They can be the famed Seville olives, sweet, meaty *manzanillas*; or *gordales*, the size of small plums, or home-cured ones, slightly bitter, flavoured with thyme, fennel and garlic, or olives stuffed with anchovy. A *tapa* of mixed olives might include fat caper-berries too.

THE *TAPAS* EXPERIENCE

Among cold dishes on the *tapa* bar are a variety of salads, some wonderfully exotic. For example, *salpicón* with chopped tomatoes, onions and peppers can include prawns and mussels or be made with chopped, cooked octopus. *Remojón* is a salad of oranges, codfish, onions and olives. While it might sound exotic, it tastes wonderful. So do roasted pepper salad, lemony potato salad, and cooked fish roe dressed with oil and lemon.

Spain is famous for its fish and shellfish and a *tapa* bar is a fine place to sample them. Fried fish, from tiny fresh anchovies (*boquerones*) and rings of tender squid (*calamares*) to chunks of fresh hake and batter-dipped prawns, are deliciously enticing. Look for *cazón en adobo*, fish marinated before frying, and *boquerones en vinagre* (or *al natural*), marinated raw anchovies. The selection of shellfish will astound you: clams and razor shells; mussels; prawns ranging in size from the tiny to the jumbo; crab, lobster, and more.

Then comes a variety of hot dishes. Some are cooked to order in individual portions, such as prawns *al ajillo*, sizzled with garlic and oil, and garlicky, grilled pork loin, while others are dished out of a bubbling stew-pot. You can savour: meatballs in almond sauce; kidneys in sherry sauce; sautéed mushrooms; chicken fried with lots and lots of garlic; lamb stew; broad beans with ham; piquant tripe; spicy snails; and, of course, *tortilla*, potato omelette. Other tasty *tapas* include fritters and croquettes crisp-fried in olive oil — Spain produces the world's finest olive oil.

Tapas make for great parties. Select a few to make a lively change from canapés, or prepare a lavish spread to serve as a buffet dinner. Most dishes can be prepared in advance, meaning you have only some last-minute preparations and re-heating. Also, many of these snacks can substitute for starters, and among the main courses are several which can be served as *tapas*. You see how versatile?

Here are a few recipes to get you started.

COLD DISHES ON THE *TAPA* BAR

SHELLFISH COCKTAIL
Salpicón de Mariscos

In Spanish *tapa* bars, this salad is also made using chopped cooked octopus instead of the shellfish. It is an attractive dish to serve for a buffet dinner, on a platter with greens and sliced avocado. Or serve it in individual portions as a starter.

> 1/2 kg/1 lb mussels, scrubbed and steamed open
> 250 g/1/2 lb peeled prawns (shrimp)
> 1/2 kg/1 lb tomatoes, chopped
> 1/2 onion, chopped
> 1 green pepper, chopped
> 1/2 cucumber, peeled and chopped (optional)
> 2 hard-cooked eggs
> 1 clove garlic, crushed
> 6 tablespoons extra virgin olive oil
> 5 tablespoons wine vinegar
> 3 tablespoons chopped parsley
> 1 teaspoon salt
> lettuce to garnish

Discard mussel shells and any mussels that do not open. If you like, save a few on the half-shell to garnish the platter. Cook the peeled prawns in boiling salted water for one minute and drain. In a bowl combine the chopped tomatoes, onion, green pepper, cucumber and chopped egg whites.

In a small bowl mash the yolks with the crushed garlic. Whisk in the olive oil, vinegar, parsley and salt. Add prawns and mussels to the tomato mixture. Stir in the dressing and chill, covered, until serving time. Serve on a platter garnished with lettuce.

Makes 12 *tapa* servings or 6 starters.

THE *TAPAS* EXPERIENCE

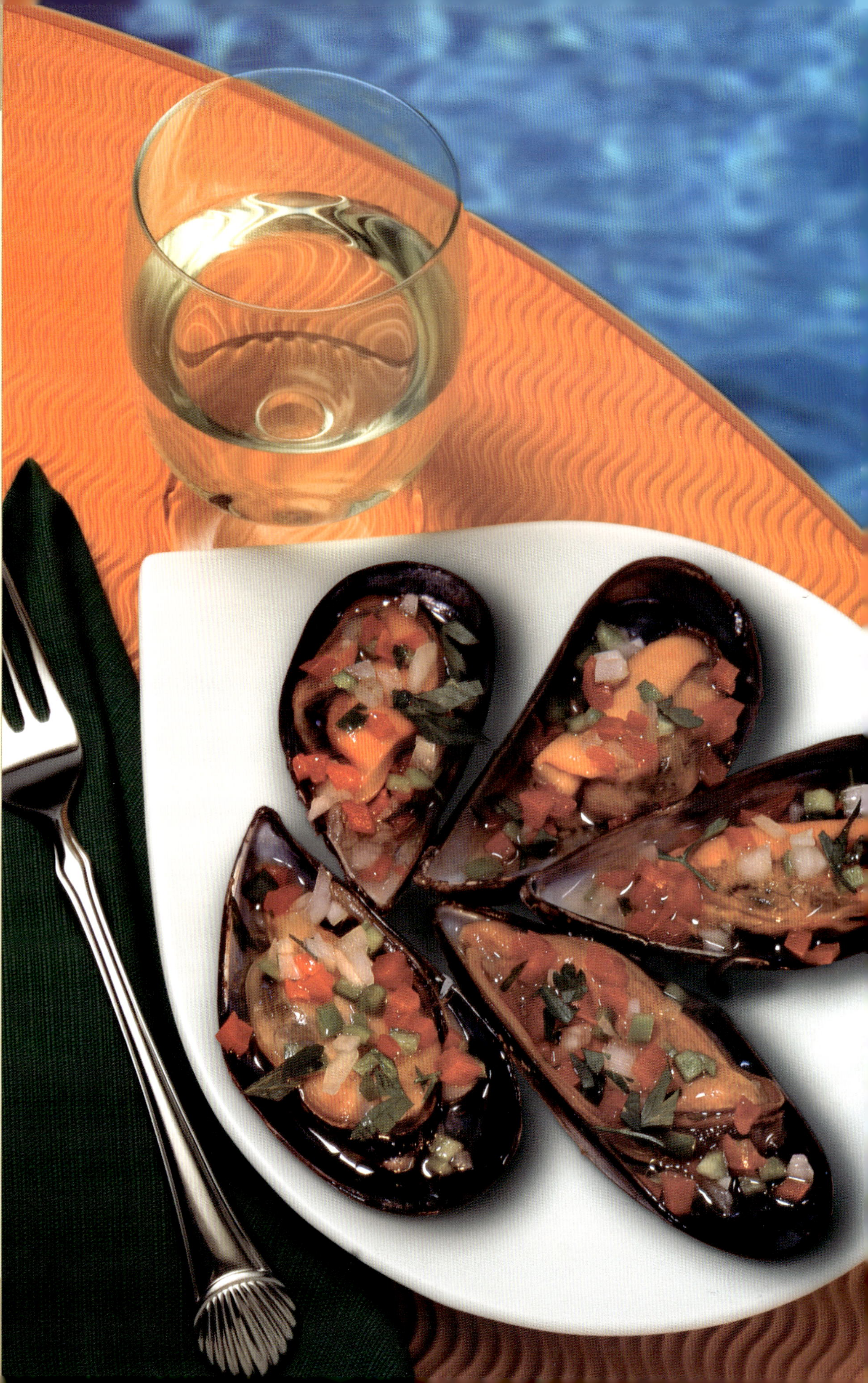

MUSSELS VINAIGRETTE
Mejillones a la Vinagreta

Galicia in northwest Spain is known for its mussel "farms" in the open sea. If you must buy mussels before the day you intend to serve them, steam them open and refrigerate, covered with their juices. Once cooked, they keep up to two days.

> 2 dozen mussels
> shredded lettuce
> 2 tablespoons minced onions
> 2 tablespoons minced green pepper
> 2 tablespoons minced red pepper
> 1 tablespoon chopped parsley
> 4 tablespoons extra virgin olive oil
> 2 tablespoons vinegar or lemon juice

Scrub the mussels, chip off any barnacles, remove the beards (the sea-weedy tuft with which they attach themselves to rocks), and rinse in running water. Put them in a deep pan with just a little water. Cover and put over a hot fire. Shake the pan until the mussel shells open, two or three minutes, removing them from heat as soon as they open. Discard any which do not open.

When the mussels have cooled, discard empty half-shells. Chill the mussels. Arrange them on a serving dish atop a bed of shredded lettuce. Combine the minced onions, green pepper, red pepper, parsley, oil and vinegar. Spoon the mixture on to the mussels in their shells.

Makes 24 *tapas*.

MARINATED FRESH ANCHOVIES
Boquerones al Natural

So different is this dish from salty, tinned anchovies that there should be another name entirely for this little fish. The fresh anchovies are filleted and marinated in vinegar to produce this *tapa* dish, which is found everywhere in Spain. If you can't get fresh anchovies, substitute thin strips of sardine, herring or mackerel.

> 1/2 kg/1 lb fresh anchovies
> 125 ml/4 fl oz (1/2 cup) white wine vinegar
> 1/2 teaspoon salt
> shredded lettuce, if desired
> 2 cloves garlic, coarsely chopped
> 2 tablespoons parsley, chopped
> 2 tablespoons extra virgin olive oil
> lemon juice

Cut off the heads and gut the fish. With a knife tip, grasp the top of the spine and pull it down across the belly to fillet the fish. Cut it off at the tail, leaving the two fillets attached by the tail. Rinse the fillets in ice water, then drain and place them in a single layer in a glass, ceramic or plastic dish. Add salt and enough vinegar to completely cover them. Cover and marinate for 24 hours or longer. The flesh will turn solid and white, cooked by the vinegar.

Before serving, rinse the fish in ice water and drain well. Arrange them on a plate, on a bed of shredded lettuce, skin side down, in spoke-fashion. Sprinkle with chopped garlic and parsley and drizzle with oil and just a touch of lemon juice. To serve the anchovies as canapés, place them on strips of bread.

Makes 12 *tapa* servings.

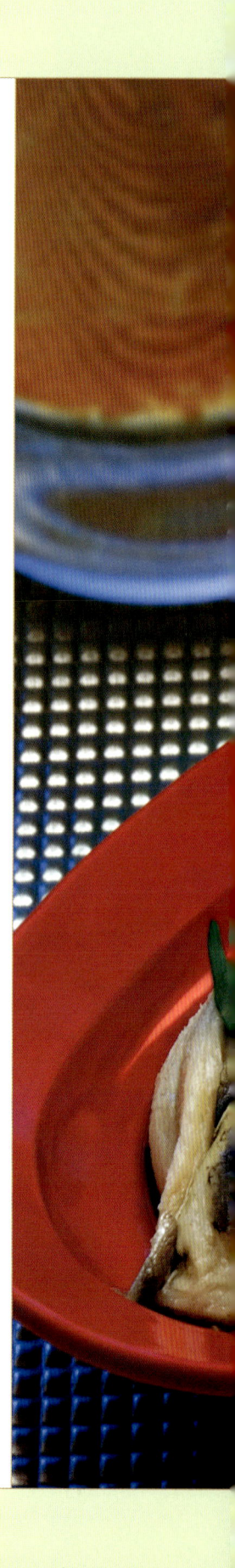

THE *TAPAS* EXPERIENCE

ROASTED PEPPER SALAD
Ensalada de Pimientos Asados

Sometimes you can buy these roasted peppers at a *panadería* (bakery), where they are roasted in the residual heat after the day's bread has baked. Their smoky-sweet fragrance wafts through a whole *barrio* (district). This salad is good as a *tapa*, as a starter or as a side dish with grilled meat, chicken or fish. It also can be served atop toasted slices of country bread and garnished with a strip of salty anchovy. Should you have any peppers left over, purée them in a blender with a little liquid or cream and use as a sauce. You can make the salad with all red capsicum (bell) peppers or, for a combination of flavour and colour, use red, green and yellow peppers.

- 6-8 sweet (bell) peppers, red and/or green and yellow
- 1 clove garlic, minced
- 3 tablespoons extra virgin olive oil
- 3 tablespoons vinegar
- salt and pepper

Roast the peppers over a gas flame, on the barbecue or under the grill (broiler), turning them frequently until charred on all sides. Remove them to a bowl and cover until they are cool enough to handle.

Peel off the skin from the peppers. Cut out the stems and seeds and discard them. Tear or cut the peppers into strips and put on a serving plate. Add the minced garlic, oil, vinegar, salt and pepper. Toss gently. The peppers can be prepared in advance and chilled, but serve the salad at room temperature.

Serves 8.

CATALAN TOMATO TOASTS
Pan amb Tomat

How could anything so simple be so delicious? Or, maybe it's not so simple — you need really good country bread, superb olive oil and the finest raw *serrano* ham. And, for sure, vine-ripened tomatoes. While this is a favourite *tapa* all over Spain, it's also served for breakfast.

> day-old bread, thickly sliced
> garlic (optional)
> ripe tomato
> extra virgin olive oil, such as Catalan *arbequina*
> thinly sliced *serrano* ham

Toast or grill the slices of bread. Rub one side of each slice with a cut clove of garlic, if desired. Then scrub the toasted bread with a cut tomato. Some people prefer to grate the tomato into pulp and spoon it onto the toasts. One way or another, you want to impregnate the toasted bread with tomato pulp. Drizzle on lots of olive oil. Top with the sliced ham.

THE *TAPAS* EXPERIENCE

BEST HAM IN THE WORLD AND SOME VERY DISTINCTIVE SAUSAGE

Some of the best *tapas* don't even require cooking—just slice and serve. That's the case with *jamón serrano*, Spanish *serrano* and *ibérico* ham, and most sausages too.

So, what's the difference between *serrano* ham and *ibérico* ham? Price, for one thing. *Ibérico* is about ten times more costly than *serrano*. That's because, though cured in a similar manner, the hams originate in different kinds of pigs. *Serrano* ham comes from cross-breeds such as Large White or Duroc, while *ibérico* comes exclusively from the *ibérico* breed. Native to western Spain, these black or brown-coloured pigs never get as hefty as regular porkers. They range through the *dehesas*, rough scrublands, feeding on wild acorns that make for incredibly sweet flesh marbled with fat. These hams are often called *pata negra*, as the pigs have black hoofs.

Serrano means "mountain", because traditionally hams were cured in mountain regions where cold winters and hot summers aided in the curing process. Nowadays, most *serrano* ham is produced in temperature-controlled factories, allowing for year-round production.

Whole hams, including the hoofs, are packed in salt for 10 to 20 days to draw out moisture. They are then washed and hung in airing rooms for several weeks, then transferred to maturing cellars for eight to 16 months for *serrano* ham and 14 to 36 months for *ibérico*. Neither type is smoked nor cooked. Nor do they contain nitrates or other preservatives.

Some hams bear guarantee of quality labels (the DO or *denominación de origen* classification) such as the *serrano* hams of Teruel and Trevélez and the *ibérico* hams from Huelva (including the famous ham-producing town of Jabugo), Dehesa de Extremadura, Pedroches and Guijuelo.

Other useful words to know when purchasing ham are: *bellota*, which designates ham from *ibérico* pigs fed on acorns; *recebo*, from pigs fed partially on acorns and finished with grains; and *cebo*, from stock reared on other types of fodder. The *bellota* hams, truly the best in the world, are considerably more expensive than the other types. *Paleta* is shoulder, which can be cured as for ham.

Cured ham is marketed whole, on the bone. The hams hang in bars, to be sliced to order. Supermarkets devote a whole aisle to their display, especially prominent at the Christmas season when Spanish families are most likely to buy them. Ham can also be purchased, hand-sliced to order, at the deli counter. Keep it tightly wrapped and refrigerated, but allow to come to room temperature before serving. Boned ham that is machine-sliced, and sometimes vacuum-packaged as well, is industrially produced ham that may contain preservatives (check the label).

How to slice *serrano* ham

Brace the ham on a special ham board. Clamp it into position with the hoof pointing down, the flat of the hoof facing downward. This presents the smaller muscle, from inside the leg, for cutting first. Because it is thinner than the back, rump muscle, it dries out faster. (If a whole ham is to be used within a few days, it does not matter which side is cut first.)

THE *TAPAS* EXPERIENCE

Use a very sharp slicing knife with a long, flexible blade.

Start by removing the outer crust and fat from the top and sides, just sufficiently to expose the meat. Save the layers of fat.

Slicing downwards from the top, with the grain of the meat, cut slices as thinly as possible, so they are almost transparent. Keep the knife almost flat against the flesh so that each slice is of even thinness. Try to cut short, wide pieces approximately 7 cm (3 inches) square. Cut long thin strips as necessary to even-up the cutting surface. Most slices should have a rim of fat (also edible).

Arrange the slices on a serving plate in a single layer, slightly overlapping, with the longer pieces placed like spokes and the smaller pieces in the center. Serve the ham immediately.

Cover the cut surfaces of the remaining ham with the reserved layers of fat and cover the ham loosely with foil, plastic wrap or a clean cloth. This prevents the exposed ham from drying out. The next time the ham is sliced, discard outer pieces if they are dry. Remove additional fat from the sides as needed.

Once the top side is sliced down to the bone, continue by cutting the butt end. Slice it crosswise instead of lengthwise. Then turn the ham over, clamp it down again, remove outer coating and fat and slice the rump side, lengthwise.

Sausage Story

Sausages (*embutidos*) turn up at *tapa* bars too. Some feature a *surtido de ibérico*, a selection of ham and sausages all made from *ibérico* pork. Here's the scoop on sausage.

Chorizo is Spain's most emblematic sausage. Made of minced pork and pork fat and well-flavoured with *pimentón* (paprika) and garlic, it comes both hard-cured, for slicing, and soft, for stewing or barbecuing. Either one might be served as a *tapa*. In Asturias, in northern Spain, smoked *chorizo* is essential to the famous bean dish, *fabada*.

Salchichón is a hard sausage for slicing, very much like salami. If it's made in a long, skinny roll, it's called *longaniza*.

Morcilla is spicy blood sausage or black pudding, with either onions or rice to plump it up and sometimes with pine kernels too. Stew it (lovely with lentils) or grill it.

Sobreasada is Mallorca's contribution to the sausage line-up. It's a soft sausage flavoured with paprika. Spread it on slabs of toasted bread.

Catalonia's choice is *butifarra blanca*, a white pork sausage that's ever so good grilled over hot coals.

Well-seasoned pork loin, stuffed in sausage casings and cured, is *lomo embuchado*, delicious sliced cold or fried up with eggs.

Cecina is salt-cured beef or venison, served in paper-thin slices with a drizzle of olive oil and a grind of fresh black pepper.

GREAT DISHES FROM SPAIN

CANARY ISLANDS WRINKLY POTATOES WITH SPICY HERB SAUCES
Papas Arrugadas con Mojo

The Canary Islands are an archipelago of seven volcanic islands situated in the Atlantic Ocean about 600 km (375 miles) southwest of continental Europe, and only 65 km (40 miles) off the coast of western Africa. Although the islands are Spanish provinces, they are closer to Morocco than Spain.

The potatoes with a spicy sauce make a good side dish with fish or grilled meats, but they also can be served as a party hors d'oeuvre. Serve them hot or at room temperature, speared with toothpicks and accompanied by dipping sauces.

> 3/4 kg/1 1/2 lbs small potatoes, not peeled
> 1 tablespoon coarse salt
> 500 ml/1 pint (2 cups) water

Place the potatoes in a pan with the salt and water. Bring to a boil and cook on a high heat until all the water has evaporated, about 20 minutes. The potatoes should be tender, coated with white salt and their skins slightly wrinkled.

If using very small new potatoes, cook them in the water just until tender when probed with a skewer. Drain off the water and return the potatoes to the heat to dry them.

Serves 8.

GREEN CHILLI SAUCE
Mojo Verde

> 2 cloves garlic
> 1 *jalapeño* chilli, or to taste
> 1/2 teaspoon ground cumin
> 1 teaspoon oregano
> 2 tablespoons chopped parsley
> large bunch (1/2 cup loosely packed) coriander (*cilantro*) leaves
> 3 tablespoons extra virgin olive oil
> 3 tablespoons wine vinegar
> 1/2 teaspoon salt
> 4 tablespoons water

Place all ingredients in a blender container and blend until smooth. Serve the sauce at room temperature. Sauce keeps one week, refrigerated.

RED CHILLI SAUCE
Mojo Colorado

> 3 tablespoons *pimentón* or paprika
> 1 fresh red chilli, seeded and chopped, or cayenne to taste
> 3 cloves garlic
> 3 tablespoons extra virgin olive oil
> 3 tablespoons wine vinegar
> 1/2 teaspoon ground cumin
> 1/2 teaspoon salt
> 4 tablespoons water

Place all of the ingredients in a blender and blend until smooth. If desired, thin with a little water. Sauce keeps one week, refrigerated.

GREAT DISHES FROM SPAIN

THE *TAPAS* EXPERIENCE

OUT OF THE FRYING PAN

HOT POTATOES
Patatas Bravas

These potatoes are hot as in chilli peppers, which go into the sauce. The original version comes from a Madrid *tapa* bar.

> For the *brava* sauce:
> 175 ml/6 fl oz (2/3 cup) tomato sauce
> 2 tablespoons extra virgin olive oil
> 1 clove garlic, crushed
> 1 tablespoon vinegar
> 1 teaspoon paprika
> 1/2 teaspoon ground cumin
> pinch of oregano
> cayenne or red pepper flakes to
>   make the sauce hot
> salt

Combine the tomato sauce, oil, garlic, vinegar, paprika, cumin, oregano, cayenne and salt.

> For the potatoes;
> 500 g/1 lb potatoes, peeled and cut in
>   3 cm (1 1/4 inch) cubes
> olive oil for frying
> salt

Fry the cubed potatoes in deep hot oil until they are golden-brown and tender (test them by piercing with a skewer), about 10 minutes. Drain them on paper towelling and sprinkle with salt. Heap the potatoes on a platter and pour the sauce over them.
Makes 8 *tapa* servings.

GREAT DISHES FROM SPAIN

MARINATED FRIED FISH
Cazón en Adobo

Many *tapa* dishes can be prepared well in advance, but those that are fried, like this one, should be served immediately. While in Spain this is usually made with *cazón* (dogfish, a kind of shark) which benefits from the tangy marinade, any solid-fleshed fish, such as angler (monkfish), works well.

> 800 g/1 3/4 lb fish fillets, such as shark or angler-fish
> 3 tablespoons olive oil
> 5 tablespoons wine vinegar
> 1 tablespoon water
> 3 cloves garlic, chopped
> 1/4 teaspoon *pimentón* (paprika)
> 1 teaspoon oregano
> 1/4 teaspoon ground black pepper
> 1/2 teaspoon salt
> flour
> olive oil for frying

Cut the fish into 4 cm/1 1/2 inch cubes, discarding any skin and bone. Put it in a glass or ceramic bowl. Mix together the oil, vinegar, water, garlic, *pimentón*, oregano, pepper and salt. Pour over the fish and mix well. Marinate for at least 6 hours or overnight.

Drain the fish well, dredge it in flour and fry the pieces a few at a time in hot oil until golden and crisp. Drain on paper towelling and serve hot.

Makes about 45 pieces.

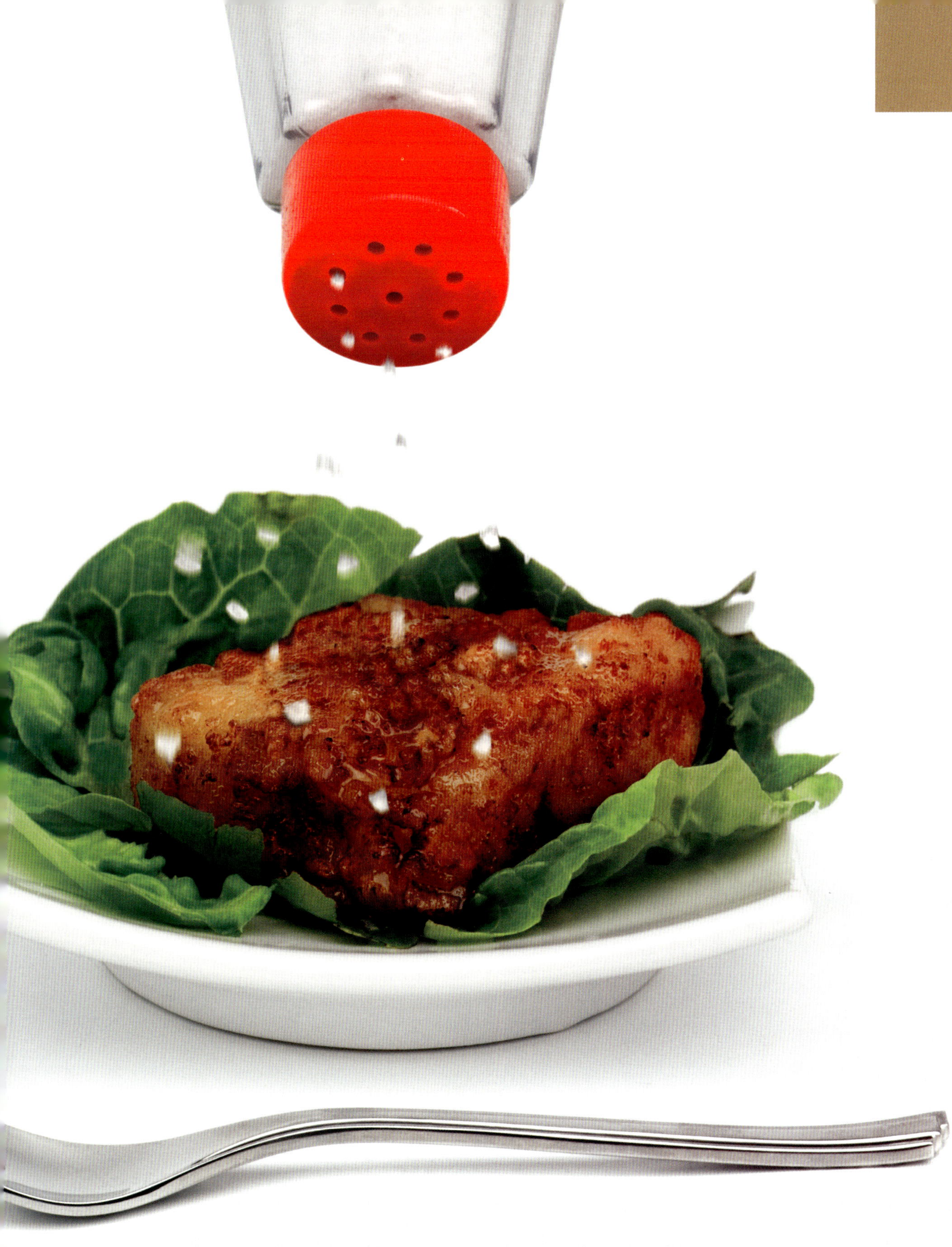

GREAT DISHES FROM SPAIN

PRAWNS IN RAINCOATS
Gambas en Gabardinas

A classic in *tapa* bars. Supposedly, the batter-dipped and fried prawns look like they're wearing coats.

> 500 g/1 lb raw jumbo prawns (shrimp), peeled, leaving the tails unpeeled
> 1 egg, beaten
> 4 tablespoons water
> 1/2 teaspoon salt
> 1/4 teaspoon bicarbonate of soda (baking soda)
> 100 g/3 oz (3/4 cup + 1 tbsp) plain flour
> olive oil for deep-frying

Combine the egg, water, salt, bicarbonate and flour to make a batter that is thick enough to coat the prawns. If necessary, thin with water, a few drops at a time.

Heat the oil to 180ºC/350ºF. Dip the prawns by their tails into the batter then fry in the hot oil. The batter should puff slightly. Remove the prawns when golden. These are good served with a spicy tomato sauce (see the recipe for the sauce with Hot Potatoes).

Makes about 10 *tapa* servings (allowing 3 prawns per person).

SPAIN'S DELECTABLE CHEESES

As *tapa*, snack, sandwich or dessert, cheese is favourite fare. Spain produces almost 100 different regional cheeses, some so distinctive that they have *denominación de origen* (DO) labels and other farmhouse cheeses made in such small quantities that they are hardly known outside their region of production. Some are produced by artisans, others on an industrial scale and widely marketed.

Spain's cheeses may be made from the milk of cows, sheep or goats or a mixture of all. In general, cows' milk cheeses come from the northern third of the country, where green pastures allow dairy cattle to thrive, sheep's milk cheeses from the central, sheep-rearing regions of Castilla-La Mancha and Castilla y León, and goats' milk cheeses from Andalusia, Extremadura and Murcia.

Serve cheese with wine or sherry and a selection of bread or crackers. Good accompaniments are fruit, walnuts, and quince jelly.

Here's a sampling.

Sheep's milk cheeses

Manchego. Produced in the central Castilla-La Mancha region, Manchego is far and away Spain's best-known cheese. So much so that imitations are dubbed "Manchego-style". Real Manchego, with DO, is made only in the designated geographical region and from the milk of ewes of the *Manchega* breed. It must be aged a minimum of 60 days, for semi-cured, producing a mild, smooth cheese with a subtle nutty aroma, delicious served on its own or used in cooking. Aged Manchego can be fairly piquant and the well-aged is splintery, strong, but mellow. It is labelled *artesanal* if made from raw milk; *industrial* cheese if made from pasteurised milk. Some cheese-makers cure whole cheeses immersed in olive oil, giving them a different flavour dimension. At *tapa* bars you may see sliced cheese preserved in a jar of oil. It's delicious with lots of bread. Genuine Manchego carries the DO (*Denominación de Origen*) quality guarantee.

Idiazábal. Made from the milk of the longhaired *latxa* sheep in the Basque Country. A robust, slightly acidic cheese that is often smoked over beech wood. DO.

Roncal. From Navarrese valleys in the Pyrenees. Aged a minimum of four months, it is buttery, earthy. DO.

La Serena and *Torta de Casar*. Both from Extremadura and both unusual in that they are made with a vegetable coagulant, a kind of thistle. La Serena is a creamy cheese, expensive because it is made in very small quantities. Torta de Casar is a soft, runny cheese with a slight bitter taste. To serve, the top rind is opened and the cheese scooped out with a spoon. DO.

Zamorano. Made in Zamora province in Castilla y León region from the milk of *churra* and *castellana* sheep. Long-aged in cellars and rubbed with oil, it is intense, nutty, slightly piquant. DO.

Goats' milk cheeses

Ibores. Made from raw goats' milk in Cáceres (Extremadura). It has a dark rind and a buttery, wild herb flavour. DO.

Majorero. From Fuerteventura in the Canary Islands. Usually rubbed with oil and *pimentón* (paprika). Acidic, a little piquant, buttery. DO.

Málaga and *Ronda*. Fresh white goats' cheese from the mountains near Ronda (Málaga). Mild, slightly salty. Also semi-cured.

Murcia al vino. From Murcia in eastern Spain, a soft, white goat cheese bathed in red wine, giving it a purple rind and a tangy flavour. DO.

Cows' milk cheeses

Burgos. Fresh, mild, moist white cheese from Burgos.

Cabrales. A blue cheese from Asturias in northern Spain. Aged in caves, it is off-white, veined with blue-green. It has a lovely creamy consistency with a "bite" to it. DO

Alt Urgell and Cerdanya. Made from pasteurised cows' milk in the Catalan Pyrenees. Amber-coloured rind and soft, creamy flesh. DO

Mahón. Made on the island of Menorca, where the dairy business is second only to tourism in economic importance. Can be fresh, semi-cured or well-aged, in which case it is quite piquant. The rind may be rubbed with oil and *pimentón* (paprika). DO.

Nata de Cantabria. Melt-in-the-mouth cream cheese with a bittersweet flavour. DO.

Picón. Cantabria. Often made with a mixture of cows', sheep's and goats' milk. Aged in caves, a blue-veined cheese. DO.

Tetilla. From Galicia in northwest Spain, the cheese is named for its shape, a lovely rounded breast. Yellow on the outside, paler on the inside, with a smooth, buttery texture. Very mild. DO. *San Simón* is a similar cheese that is smoked, giving it a darker rind and smoky flavour.

Valdeón. A smooth and mild blue cheese from the Picos de Europa area of León. A cows' milk cheese that sometimes has goats' milk added. DO.

Villalón. A soft, fresh mild cheese from Castilla y León.

GREAT DISHES FROM SPAIN

FROM THE KITCHEN

SPANISH POTATO OMELETTE
Tortilla Española

A *tortilla* is a big golden disk, which can be cut into wedges or squares to be served as a *tapa*. It also makes a nice supper dish. The classic tortilla is made with potatoes, but other vegetables can be incorporated. Try aubergine (eggplant) or chopped chard with the potatoes.

> 6 tablespoons olive oil
> 1 kg/2lbs potatoes, peeled and thinly sliced
> 2 tablespoons chopped onion
> 6 eggs
> 1 teaspoon salt

Heat the oil in a no-stick or well-seasoned frying pan (24-26 cm/9-10 in). Add the sliced potatoes and turn them in the oil. Let them cook slowly in the oil, without browning, turning frequently. When they are partially cooked, add the chopped onion. The potatoes will take 20 to 30 minutes to cook.

Beat the eggs in a bowl with the salt. Place a plate over the potatoes and drain off excess oil into another heatproof bowl. Add the potatoes to the beaten eggs and combine well. Add a little of the reserved oil to the frying pan and pour in the potato-egg mixture. Cook on a medium heat until set, without letting the omelette get too brown on the bottom, about 5 minutes. Shake the pan to keep the tortilla from sticking. Place a flat lid or plate over the pan, hold it tightly, and reverse the *tortilla* on to the plate. Add a little more oil to the pan, if necessary, and slide the *tortilla* back in to cook on the reverse side, about 3 minutes more. Slide out onto a serving plate. Serve hot or cold.

Cut into squares, makes 15-20 *tapa* servings, or, sliced, 4 luncheon or supper servings.

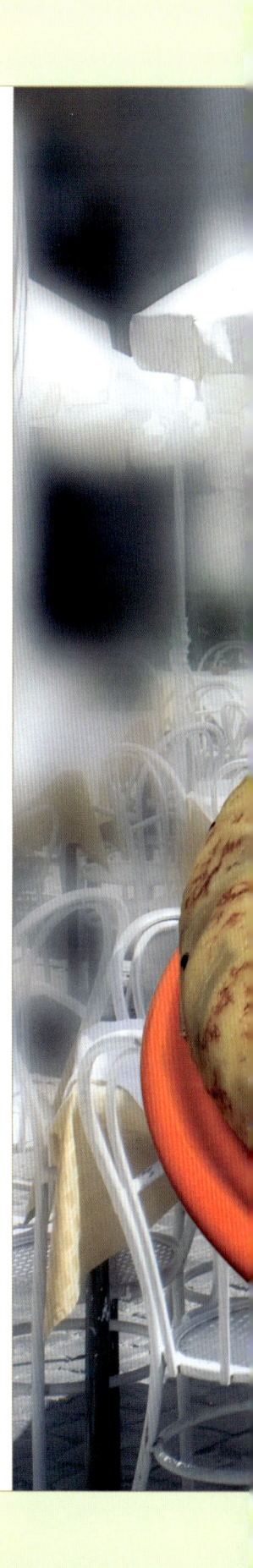

THE *TAPAS* EXPERIENCE

GREAT DISHES FROM SPAIN

THE *TAPAS* EXPERIENCE

SPICY PORK KEBABS
Pinchitos Morunos

These kebabs are flavoured with a spice blend from North Africa, consisting of lots of cumin with coriander, turmeric, ginger, pepper, and cayenne. You can make a similar blend by combining cumin with curry powder. Cut the meat into very small cubes, so that it cooks through very quickly. After marinating, thread it on thin metal skewers. Grill over charcoal or on a *plancha*, a flat griddle.

> 1 kg/2 lbs boneless pork shoulder
> 1 tablespoon ground cumin
> 1 tablespoon curry powder
> 1/2 teaspoon cayenne (or to taste)
> 4 tablespoons chopped flat-leaf parsley
> 10 garlic cloves, chopped
> 2 teaspoons salt
> 100 ml/3 1/2 fl oz (1/3 cup) fresh lemon juice
> olive oil
> bread for serving

Trim the meat of any connective tissue and fat. Cut it into small cubes (2 1/2 cm/1 inch). Combine the cumin, curry powder and cayenne in a small bowl.

Layer the cubes of pork with the parsley, garlic, salt, spice mixture and lemon juice. Cover and refrigerate for 8 to 24 hours. Turn the meat two or three times.

Thread four pieces of meat onto 18-20 thin metal skewers (or wooden skewers that have been soaked in water).

Heat a griddle or unridged grill pan and brush with oil. (The kebabs also may be cooked on a charcoal grill.)

Brush the kebabs with oil and grill them, turning two or three times, until browned on all sides, 7-8 minutes. Serve the kebabs immediately with a cube of bread stuck on the end of each skewer.

Yields 20 kebabs.

GREAT DISHES FROM SPAIN

GARLIC-SIZZLED PRAWNS
Gambas al Ajillo

In *tapa* bars this is usually prepared in *cazuelitas*, individual earthenware ramekins, that come to the table really sizzling. Take care you don't burn your tongue! The ramekins can be used right on a gas or electric hob (burner). Just take care not to set them on a cold surface. If you prepare the prawns in a frying pan, as in the following recipe, the prawns lose their sizzle when transferred to serving dishes. But they taste just as delicious as the *tapa* bar version. Serve the prawns with lots of bread for dunking into the garlicky sauce.

> 40 medium peeled and deveined prawns (shrimp), about 225 g/8 oz
> 8 tablespoons olive oil
> 4 cloves garlic, sliced crosswise
> 4 slices dried chilli pepper
> 2 tablespoons water
> pinch of *pimentón* (paprika)
> pinch of coarse salt
> bread for serving

Rinse the prawns and pat them dry. Heat the oil in a frying pan until it is shimmering, but not smoking. Add the garlic and chilli and cook until garlic begins to colour, 30 seconds. Add the prawns in a single layer. Cook them, stirring, until they turn pink, 30 to 40 seconds.

Remove the pan from the heat. Stir in the water. Sprinkle with *pimentón* and salt. Spoon the prawns, garlic and juices into 4 individual ramekins. Serve with bread.

Serves 4 as a *tapa*.

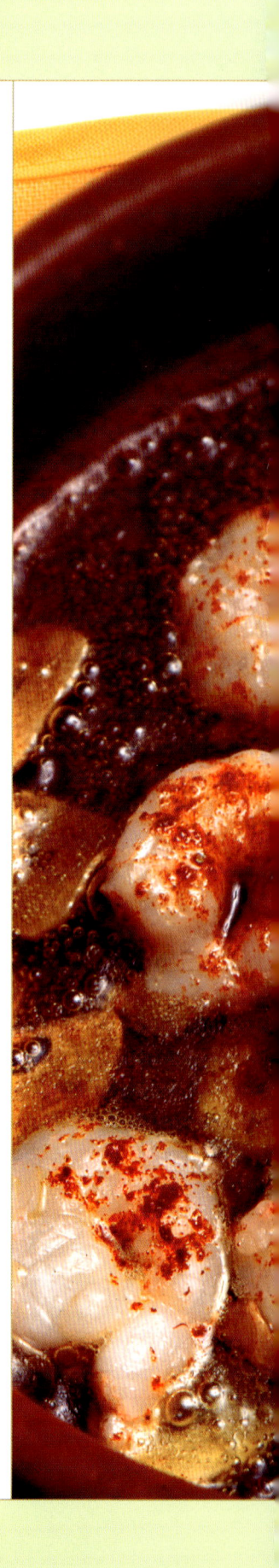

THE *TAPAS* EXPERIENCE

SIPPING SPAIN: WHAT TO DRINK WITH TAPAS, WITH DINNER

There's no better accompaniment to most *tapa* foods than *fino* or *manzanilla*, both fresh, dry sherries, from Jerez de la Frontera and nearby Sanlúcar de Barrameda in Andalusia. They are the perfect match to toasted almonds, Spanish ham, olives, most cheese, prawns, fried foods, kidneys and meatballs. Sherry, a fortified wine, has a higher alcohol content (more than 15.5 percent) than table wines. Another good reason for those tidbits of food. Serve *fino* and *manzanilla* chilled.

Amontillado is a more mellow sherry, still dry, but with a nutty flavour that *aficionados* adore. Enjoy it with aged cheese, nuts, smoked meats, sausage, mushrooms, and chicken dishes.

Looking beyond sherry, you'll discover some terrific wine choices to go with Spanish *tapa*s and favourite dishes: red, or *tinto*; white, *blanco*; rosé, *rosado*; and sparkling, *cava*.

Spain has the most extensive vineyards in the world and only France produces a larger volume of wine. The numbers are huge, but not just on the quantity scale. Spanish wines are also achieving the highest rankings from leading wine critics. There's a wine for every taste, to match every dish and in every price range.

Any *tapa* bar offers one or more "house" wines that can be ordered by the glass, while in wine country, such as La Rioja, bars provide dozens of tasting choices by the glass. Specialty wine bars and restaurants with their own cellars may show you a wine list with hundreds of selections to be ordered by the bottle. A wine list (and supermarket shelves) is usually organised first by colour (white, red, rosé) and then by regional denomination.

How to choose? Let's take a look at a wine label to learn the lingo.

The bottle will state the name of the wine and the *bodega*, or winery, that produced it. Sometimes the wine's name is the same as the bodega.

It may also name a DO, *denominación de origen*, the Spanish form of *appellation contrôlée* which designates the wine's geographic region and certain quality guarantees as well. The best-known DO is La Rioja, a region in northern Spain famed for the quality of its wines. But don't get stuck in a Rioja rut — try some fabulous wines from other regions. Here are some DOs to look for: Chacolí from the Basque Country; Jumilla (Murcia); La Mancha and Valdepeñas in central Spain; Navarra, adjoining Rioja; Penedés, between Barcelona and Tarragona in Catalonia; Priorato, inland Catalonia; Rías Baixas from Galicia in northwest Spain; Ribera del Duero, Toro and Rueda, all on the River Duero in the region of Castilla y León; Somontano and Cariñena in Aragón; Utiel-Requena from Valencia. There are more, so be adventurous and sip your way round all of Spain's wine regions. Besides DO, another classification is Vino de la Tierra (VT), which often encompasses new-generation wines that don't fit the DO's tight geographic and vinification specifications. DO Cava designates not a geographic region but sparkling wines made by the champagne method (although much of it comes from Catalonia).

The next bit of useful information on

THE *TAPAS* EXPERIENCE

the label concerns the grape varietal (not always stated). You'll see familiar names such as *cabernet sauvignon*, *syrah* and *chardonnay*, which, although not native varieties, are now widely grown in Spain. For sure you'll find wines made with *tempranillo*, Spain's best-known varietal for red wines and the basis of DO Rioja reds. Often *tempranillo* is blended with other varieties, such as *garnacha*, *mazuelo*, *graciano*. The most outstanding white-wine grape is the *albariño*, grown in northwest Galicia (DO Rías Baixas). Others are *macabeo* (also called *viura*), *parellada*, *airén*, *xarello* and *verdejo*.

Lastly, a wine label will indicate whether or not a wine has been aged. Most Spanish wine regions classify red wine vintages as *jóven*, young; *crianza*, slightly aged; *reserva*, aged; and *gran reserva*, long aged. Wines with denomination labels must adhere to minimum ageing requirements. For example, DO Rioja specifies that *crianza* wines must be in their third year, with at least one year in oak barrels. *Reserva* wines must be three years old with at least 12 months in oak, while *gran reserva* requires the wine to be aged two years in oak and three in bottle. (Other DOs may have somewhat different qualifications.)

Young wines, marked only with the year of the *cosecha*, harvest, are meant to be drunk within a year of the time they are made. Good ones are fruity and fresh, with a bright, cherry colour. They are a perfect choice with most *tapas*, especially with potato *tortilla*, meatballs, and Spanish sausages such as *chorizo*; with family meals of lentils, beans, chickpeas or pasta; with *paella*; with breaded veal or pork cutlet; with roast chicken or turkey.

Crianza wines, with just a touch of oak, go especially well with cheese of all sorts. This is also the perfect wine with most meat dishes such as grilled steak or roast pork or lamb. Serve it with hamburger of choice beef.

A *reserva* wine means "reserved", a term used to distinguish the finest wines of a vintner's cellar that are reserved, in bottle, until they are at their optimum for drinking. These wines, usually of a deep brick color, offer complex bouquet and taste. Choose them to accompany dishes such as stewed partridge, venison, duck, and beef.

White wines are most likely to be young, fresh, fruity and with light acidity, although some whites are barrel-fermented or passed briefly through oak, giving them a more complex bouquet. A chilled white wine is just what you want to go with Spain's magnificent seafood dishes. Rosé, too, is at its best when young and fresh (and is a very good choice with *paella*).

Cava (please don't call it champagne) is the celebration drink for toasting grand occasions, but makes a delightful aperitif with hors d'oeuvres (classy *tapas*). Even finest *reserva cavas* are quite reasonably priced on the home market.

Oh yes, beer goes down just fine with *tapas*. Spanish beer is light lager. You can order draught beer in most taverns—a *caña* is a short glass; *tubo* is a tall one; *jarra* is a pitcher.

Sangría, made with red wine, liqueur or brandy, sugar, and fresh fruits, is too sweet to accompany dinner, but makes a fun libation for a party. It's usually diluted with soda water or *gaseosa*, fizzy lemonade.

With the dessert course, try one of Spain's sweet wines, such as *pedro ximénez* (that's the name of the grape — the wine can come from various DOs); *oloroso* sherry, or Málaga moscatel. For after-dinner sipping, there's Brandy de Jerez, aged in sherry casks, or *aguardiente* (anisette), both dry (*seco*) and sweet (*dulce*). *Pacharán*, a digestive flavoured with sloe berries, is usually served over ice.

RED WINE FRUIT PUNCH
Sangría

A fun party drink. Use any combination of fruit in the *sangría*. Strawberries, oranges, lemons, melon, apples, pears, bananas, grapes and peaches, sliced or chopped, are some of the best. Add ice if you like.

> 50 g /2 oz (1/4 cup) sugar
> Strip of orange zest
> 250 ml/1/2 pint (1 cup) water
> 2 cups chopped or sliced fruit
> 4 tablespoons brandy or liqueur such as Cointreau
> 1 bottle chilled red wine
> chilled soda water

Combine the sugar in a small saucepan with the zest and water. Bring to a boil and simmer two minutes. Allow the sugar syrup to cool. Strain it into a pitcher. Discard the orange zest.

Add the fruit and brandy to the pitcher. The fruit can macerate, refrigerated, up to two hours. Add the chilled red wine. Immediately before serving, add chilled soda water to taste.

Serve the *sangría* and fruit in juice glasses or goblets.

Serves 8-10.

THE *TAPAS* EXPERIENCE

2
starters, soups & sides

*T*apas turn into starters and starters become main dishes. Vegetable side dishes turn up as topping for toasts at elegant *tapa* bars. And some main dishes, like that garlicky chicken sauté, *pollo al ajillo*, are classic *tapas*. While most *gazpachos* and soups are best as a starter, hearty *potajes* (stews) with pulses (legumes) make a substantial main course. Don't fancy eggs for supper? Serve them for breakfast.

The message is: combine these dishes any way you like to create appetising meals and snacks.

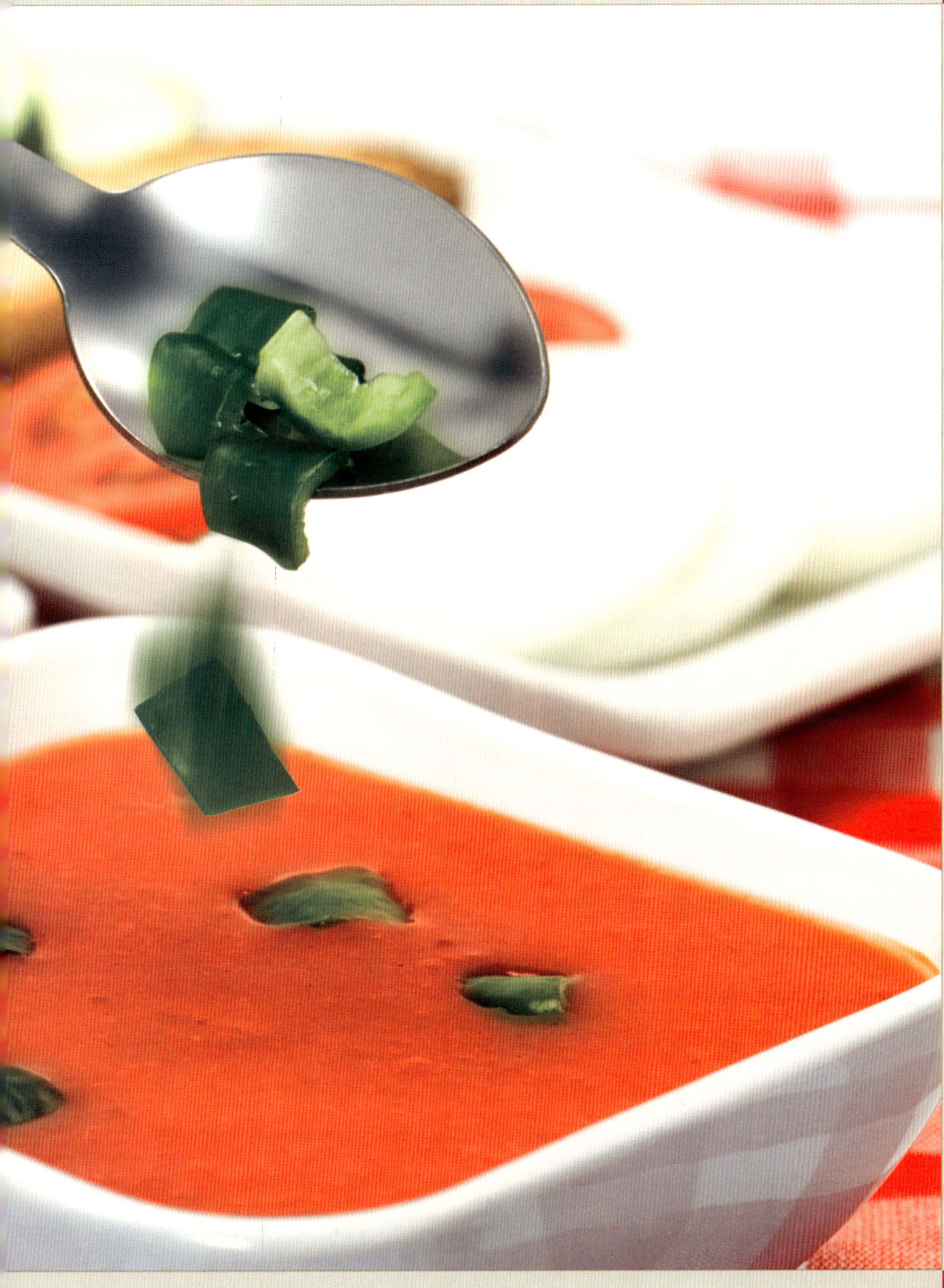

STARTERS

ORANGE AND COD SALAD
Remojón

The codfish used in this salad is *bacalao*, dry salt cod, which is immensely popular in Spain. In this recipe, it does not have to be presoaked. If salt cod is not available, you could substitute tinned tuna, cooked prawns (shrimp) or even strips of *serrano* ham. This salad makes a festive starter for a holiday meal.

> 150 g/5 oz dry salt cod
> 4-6 oranges, peeled and sliced
> 1 onion, thinly sliced (red onion if possible)
> 1 clove garlic, crushed
> 4 tablespoons extra virgin olive oil
> 1 tablespoon sherry vinegar
> pinch of red pepper flakes (optional)
> 20 green or black olives

Toast the salt cod over a flame or under the grill (broiler) until it is lightly browned and softened. Put it in a bowl of water while preparing the remaining ingredients, at least 30 minutes and up to two hours.

Arrange the orange and onion slices on a plate. Whisk the garlic with the oil, vinegar and red pepper flakes. Drain the cod and remove all skin and bones. Shred it and add to the salad. Drizzle the dressing over the salad and garnish with the olives.

Serves 6.

STARTERS, SOUPS & SIDES

GALICIAN PORK PIE
Empanada Gallega

In Galicia, the region in the top, north-west corner of Spain, these huge pies are filled with all manner of ingredients: meat, chicken, fish, clams or scallops. A great snack — and also perfect fare for a picnic in the countryside.

For the dough:
40 g/1 1/2 oz fresh yeast
150 ml/1/4 pint (3/4 cup) very warm water
1 teaspoon sugar
450 g/1 lb (3 3/4 cups) bread flour, plus additional for board
1 teaspoon salt
6 tablespoons olive oil
1 egg, beaten

Dissolve the yeast in the water. Beat in the sugar and three tablespoons of the flour. Put the yeast mixture in a warm, draft-free place for 15 minutes, or until very bubbly.

Place the remaining flour in a large bowl and add the salt. Make a well in the centre and pour in the oil and egg. Then add the yeast mixture. Gradually work the flour into the liquid ingredients. Turn out on a board and knead the dough, for at least five minutes, until it is smooth and shiny.

Put the dough in an oiled bowl, turning to coat both sides with oil. Cover with a dampened kitchen towel and place in a warm place to rise. The dough should double in bulk, about one hour.

STARTERS, SOUPS & SIDES

For the filling and baking:
350 g/3/4 lb thinly sliced pork loin
4 tablespoons olive oil
1/2 teaspoon *pimentón* (paprika)
1 teaspoon salt
2 onions, chopped
3 cloves garlic, chopped
4 tomatoes, peeled and chopped
1 tablespoon chopped parsley
1 teaspoon oregano
salt and pepper
150 ml/1/4 pint (2/3 cup) white wine
1 small tin red peppers, drained and cut in strips (*piquillo*, if available)
2 hard-boiled eggs, sliced
1 egg, beaten

Fry the pork slices in half the oil and set them aside on a plate. Sprinkle them with paprika and salt. Add the remaining oil to the pan and in it fry the chopped onions and garlic until softened. Add the tomatoes and fry until they are reduced to a sauce. Add the oregano, salt and pepper and wine. Cook until sauce is reduced, about 15 minutes.

Divide the raised dough in half. Keep one half covered. Roll the other half out to a diameter of 30 cm/12 in. It will have a thickness of about 1 cm/1/3 inch. Fit it into a large pie tin. (Or, shape the dough into a rectangle and fit it into a large oven tin.) Spread the dough with half the prepared tomato sauce. Arrange the slices of pork on top, then strips of *pimiento* and sliced egg. Cover with remaining sauce. Roll out remaining dough and cover the pie. Trim excess dough around the edges and crimp the edges together. Use the trimmings to roll into thin cords and decorate the top of the pie. Cut a steam vent in the centre. Paint the dough with beaten egg.

Bake the pie in a preheated medium-hot oven (190°C/375°F) until golden on top, about 35 minutes. Serve hot or cold.

Serves 8.

STARTERS, SOUPS & SIDES

GASTRONOMIC SOUVENIRS

Spanish markets and supermarkets are excellent places to shop for souvenirs. Gourmet foods make fine gifts for friends back home and will inspire you to experiment with typical dishes in your own kitchen. (If travelling outside the EU, check customs regulations, as some countries prohibit the entry of meats, dairy products and unprocessed fruits and vegetables.)

Tuck tins of *piquillo* peppers in the corners of your suitcase. These peppers, which come from La Rioja and Navarre, are small (7 1/2 cm/3 inch), triangular red ones that end in a *pico* or "beak". They are sweet and mildly piquant. Roasted and peeled, they are packed in tins (cans). Stuff them, use them for salads, or purée them to make a delicious sauce.

Spanish olives are world famous. Best-known are fat, Seville *manzanillas*, which are widely exported. Deliciously addictive are olives stuffed with anchovies, almonds, *pimiento* or ham. Do try the home-cured style, redolent of herbs and garlic. If you purchase olives from open stock to take back home, drain off all the liquid, then seal in plastic bags and put in plastic containers (so they don't leak in your luggage). When you get the olives home, put them in jars and cover with a strong brine. Refrigerate and they will keep for weeks—though you'll probably find your friends will devour them long before.

Along with olives, grab some capers too. Capers are the pickled flower buds of the caper bush, a sensational seasoning for fish and sauces. Caper berries are the "fruit" (seed pod). Look for tiny pickled aubergines (eggplant), called *berenjenas de Almagro*, and pickled garlic, so mild you can pop whole cloves in your mouth straight from the jar.

Friends abroad are always delighted to receive a little "taste of Spain". Try them on something a little unusual, like squid in its own ink or octopus in tomato sauce, both available in tins. Or choose pickled mussels, tuna in extra virgin olive oil, brined clams or sardines in piquant sauce, all in handy-to-pack tins.

Another outstanding product is *mojama*, "ham of the sea", which is air-dried tuna, usually found in vacuum-sealed packs. You serve it as an aperitif, sliced paper thin and drizzled with extra virgin olive oil.

Look for tinned partridge and venison pâté in gourmet shops and some supermarkets. These are made in regions of the country, such as La Mancha, where wild game is abundant.

Spain grows distinctive varieties of rice, special for *paella*. They are medium-short, round grain that soak up all the delicious cooking flavours. Look for those from Valencia and Calasparra. One variety, *bomba*, is especially esteemed—and expensive. And, should you develop a taste for the Asturian bean dish, *fabada*, you surely will want to pick up a supply of the fat white beans necessary for an authentic version.

Cooks just love receiving kitchenware and cooking utensils. Colourful pottery, earthenware casseroles and terrines, though heavy, make wonderful gifts. Look for wood or brass mortar and pestle, *paella* pans, *pinchito* skewers, olive wood bowls, wooden olive dippers, colourful pitchers for *sangría*.

53

EGGS SCRAMBLED WITH MUSHROOMS, PRAWNS AND GREEN GARLIC
Huevos Revueltos Con Setas, Gambas y Ajetes

This dish can be served as a starter or as a light supper dish. Green garlic shoots, which look like miniature spring onions, have an amazingly mild flavour. In Spain this dish is made with any one of several types of wild mushrooms, but you could use cultivated white mushrooms instead.

> 150 g/5 oz mushrooms (such as chanterelles, oyster mushrooms or *boletus*)
> 6-8 green garlic shoots
> 3 tablespoons olive oil
> 150 g/5 oz peeled and deveined raw prawns (shrimp)
> 1 tablespoon water
> 6 eggs
> salt and pepper
> squares of fried bread

Cut away any woody parts of the mushrooms, rinse under running water and pat them dry on a kitchen towel. Slice the mushrooms. Trim off ends of garlic shoots and chop them. Heat the oil in a frying pan and sauté the mushrooms and garlic until softened. Add the prawns and sauté one minute.

    Beat together the water, eggs and salt and pepper. Pour into the mushrooms and cook, stirring, until eggs are set creamy-soft. Serve immediately with fried bread.

    Serves 4 as a starter.

STARTERS, SOUPS & SIDES

GREAT DISHES FROM SPAIN

STARTERS, SOUPS & SIDES

BAKED EGGS FLAMENCO STYLE
Huevos a la Flamenca

If serving this as a starter, allow one egg per person, dividing the ingredients among eight ramekins. As a brunch or supper dish, use two eggs per person and four ramekins.

> olive oil
> 325 ml/11 fl oz (1 1/3 cups) tomato sauce
> 100 g/3 1/2 oz ham, chopped
> 8 eggs
> 2 tablespoons cooked peas
> strips of tinned red *pimiento*
> slices of *chorizo* sausage
> 8 asparagus tips, cooked or tinned
> salt and pepper
> chopped parsley

Oil four or eight individual ovenproof ramekins and divide the tomato sauce between them. Sprinkle a little chopped ham into each. Break one or two eggs into each ramekin. Sprinkle on a few cooked peas, criss-cross the top with strips of *pimiento*, and set a *chorizo* slice next to the eggs. Top with asparagus tips. Sprinkle with salt and pepper and chopped parsley.

Bake in a preheated medium-hot oven (200ºC/400ºF) until whites are set but yolks still liquid, about eight minutes.

Makes 8 starters or 4 supper servings.

PEPPERS STUFFED WITH FISH
Pimientos de Piquillo Rellenos con Pescado

This turns up in the trendiest *tapa* bars in Madrid and the Basque Country and also as a starter in many restaurants. *Piquillo* peppers are a special Spanish red pepper, small, sweet and slightly piquant, with pointed tips. In Spain, you can buy them in tins, already skinned and ready for stuffing. If *piquillo* peppers are not available, use very small red capsicums (bell) peppers, roasted and peeled (for how-to, see the recipe for Roasted Pepper Salad).

- 2 tins (cans) *piquillo* peppers, each 185 g/6 1/2 oz (about 15 small peppers)
- 200 g/7 oz salt cod (*bacalao*), soaked for 24 hours, or any cooked white fish
- 3 cloves garlic, chopped
- 1 tablespoon onion, minced
- 2 tablespoons olive oil
- 1 1/2 tablespoons flour
- 200 ml/7 fl oz (3/4 cup + 1 tbsp) milk
- salt and pepper to taste
- grating of nutmeg
- 150 ml/1/4 pint (2/3 cup) cream
- pinch of cayenne
- 1 teaspoon vinegar

Drain the tinned *piquillo* peppers. Allow 12 for stuffing and reserve the remainder with the juice for the sauce. Shred or flake the soaked codfish or cooked white fish, discarding any skin or bone.

In a saucepan, sauté the chopped garlic and onion in the oil until softened. Add the flour and cook for two minutes. Then whisk in the milk. Season with salt and pepper and nutmeg. Cook, stirring constantly, until the mixture is thickened. Stir in the cod or fish. Remove from heat.

Stuff the *piquillo* peppers with the fish mixture and place them in an oiled baking dish. Bake in a medium-hot oven for five minutes. (Alternatively, the peppers may be dusted with flour, then dipped in beaten egg and fried in olive oil, turning them to brown on all sides.)

Meanwhile, purée the remaining peppers and liquid in a blender with the cream, cayenne and vinegar. Spoon the sauce onto individual dishes and place two stuffed peppers on top.

Serves 4-6 as a starter.

STARTERS, SOUPS & SIDES

GREAT DISHES FROM SPAIN

GRILLED PRAWNS WITH ROMESCO SAUCE
Langostinos a la Plancha con Salsa de Romesco

Romesco is a sensational Catalan sauce. It's particularly good with grilled fish and shellfish, but it can accompany any grilled meat or poultry or, thinned with a bit of water, serve as a dressing for vegetables or salads. The sauce is named for a type of dried sweet red pepper, which gives it a characteristic ruddy colour. North Americans have several similar peppers (not hot chillies). Otherwise, substitute an extra spoonful of paprika.

> large, unpeeled *langostinos* (king prawns or jumbo shrimp)
> 4-5 small dried sweet red peppers (*ñoras*) or 2 tablespoons *pimentón* (paprika)
> 1 chilli pepper or to taste
> 3 tomatoes
> 1 head of garlic
> 1 dozen almonds, blanched and skinned
> 2 dozen hazelnuts, skinned
> 25 g/1 oz (1 slice) bread, toasted
> 1 tablespoon parsley
> 150 ml/1/4 pint (2/3 cup) extra virgin olive oil
> 1 teaspoon salt
> 1 tablespoon vinegar
> freshly ground black pepper

If using the dried peppers, remove stems and seeds and either toast and grind them or else soak in boiling water and scrape the pulp from the skins. Do the same with the chilli.

Roast the tomatoes and garlic in a hot oven until the tomato skins split, about 15 minutes. Remove. Skin the tomatoes, cut them in half and remove seeds. Skin all the garlic cloves. Put the peppers (or *pimentón*) in a blender or food processor with the tomatoes, garlic, almonds, hazelnuts, bread, parsley and part of the olive oil. Process until you have a smooth purée. Beat in remaining oil, salt, vinegar and pepper. The sauce should be the consistency of thick cream. If too thick, thin with a little water or white wine. The *romesco* sauce can be made in advance. Bring it to room temperature before serving.

Makes about 300 ml/1/2 pint of sauce, enough to accompany three dozen prawns.

Grill the prawns on a hot griddle that has been brushed with oil and sprinkled with coarse salt. They need only 2-3 minutes on each side, depending on size. Serve accompanied by the sauce — and finger bowls for after peeling the prawns. To make a meal of it, prepare a mixed grill of prawns, fish fillets, clams and mussels.

OCTOPUS, GALICIAN STYLE
Pulpo a la Gallega

If you can find frozen, cooked octopus, this is an easy dish to prepare. Otherwise, octopus needs about two hours' cooking time to become tender.

> 500 g/1 lb frozen, cooked octopus, thawed
> 2 large potatoes, boiled, peeled, and cut in chunks
> coarse salt

chopped garlic (optional)
1 tablespoon *pimentón* (paprika)
100 ml/3 1/2 fl oz (1/3 cup) extra virgin olive oil

Use scissors to cut the cooked octopus into bite-size pieces. Place them on a dish (typically a wooden dish in Galicia) with chunks of the potato. Sprinkle with coarse salt, chopped garlic and *pimentón*. Then drizzle over the oil. Serve at room temperature.

Serves 4-6 as a *tapa* or starter.

CLAMS, FISHERMEN'S STYLE
Almejas a la Marinera

You will be amazed at the variety of shellfish to be found in Spanish *tapa* bars. Ten or more sorts — crustaceans and molluscs plus some odd ones, such as barnacles — each prepared in several different manners. Some of the best are the most simple, such as this way with clams — which, by the way, can be used with mussels as well.

Use any small steamer clam or wedge-shell clam. The big Venus-shell clams, with their beautiful polished shells, aren't suitable for this dish, as they toughen with cooking. They are more appropriately served raw on the half-shell.

In *tapa* bars these clams are frequently served from a communal platter. Go right ahead, dip your chunk of bread into the delicious, garlicky juice.

> 1/2 kg/1 lb small clams
> 1 tablespoon chopped onion
> 2 cloves chopped garlic
> 3 tablespoons olive oil
> 6 tablespoons white wine
> 6 tablespoons water
> piece of chilli pepper (optional)
> 1 bay leaf
> 2 tablespoons chopped parsley

Wash the clams in running water. Discard any that are opened or cracked.

In a deep frying pan, fry the chopped onion and garlic in the oil for a few minutes until onion is softened. Add the clams. On a high heat, add the wine, water, chilli and bay leaf. Cover and shake the pan vigorously until the clamshells open. This takes three to four minutes. Remove from heat when most of shells have opened. (Discard any unopened clams.) Pour into a serving dish and top with chopped parsley. Serve with chunks of bread to dunk into the clam juices.

Serves 8 as a shared *tapa*, or 2 or 3 as a starter.

STARTERS, SOUPS & SIDES

GREAT DISHES FROM SPAIN

STARTERS, SOUPS & SIDES

GAZPACHOS AND SOUPS

Every region of Spain boasts super soups. Some are light and refreshing, like summertime *gazpacho*, made with raw ingredients. Others are heart-warming *potajes*, a stew chock-full of pulses, vegetables, meat and sausage. There are dozens of seafood soups as well. Here is an introduction to some of the greats.

COLD ANDALUSIAN TOMATO SOUP
Gazpacho Andaluz

Gazpacho is simple peasant food, the sort of midday dish made in the fields, which requires only raw vegetables, bread, garlic and olive oil. Its goodness depends on big, juicy, vine-ripened tomatoes. Serve it in bowls accompanied by chopped cucumbers, onions and peppers to garnish or in tall glasses, without the garnishes, to be sipped. On a hot summer's day, it really hits the spot.

- 75 g/2 1/2 oz (3 slices) stale bread (not packaged sandwich bread)
- 1 kg/2 lbs (4 large) ripe tomatoes
- 3 cloves garlic
- 2 teaspoons salt
- 6 tablespoons extra virgin olive oil
- 5 tablespoons vinegar
- approximately 300 ml/1/2 pint (1 1/4 cups) water

For the garnishes:
- 100 g/3 1/2 oz green pepper (1 small bell pepper), finely chopped
- 200 g/7oz cucumber (1/2 cucumber), peeled and finely chopped
- 1 small onion, finely chopped
- 1 small tomato, finely chopped
- 50 g/1 3/4 oz (2 slices) bread, diced and fried crisp in a little olive oil

Put the bread to soak in enough water to cover for 10 minutes. Squeeze out excess water and discard crusts.

Purée the tomatoes in a blender or food processor. Sieve the pulp to remove all skin and seeds. Put the garlic in a blender or processor and chop finely. Add the bread, then the tomato pulp. (If necessary, process in two batches.) With the motor running, add the salt, then the oil in a slow stream, then the vinegar. The mixture will thicken and change colour as the oil emulsifies. Add a little of the water and transfer to a serving bowl or pitcher. Add additional water to desired consistency — *gazpacho* is usually as thick as pouring cream. Chill until serving time.

Arrange the garnishes in separate bowls and serve with the *gazpacho*. Each person adds the accompaniments to taste.

Serves 5-6.

COLD WHITE GARLIC SOUP WITH GRAPES
Ajo Blanco con Uvas

This version of *gazpacho*, typical of Málaga, is made with finely ground almonds instead of tomatoes. Sweet muscatel grapes make a marvellous counterpoint to the tangy, garlicky soup. Unusual and very sophisticated.

> 200 g/7 oz (6-8 slices) stale bread, crusts removed
> 200 g/7 oz (1 1/2 cups) almonds, blanched and skinned
> 3 cloves garlic
> 150 ml/1/4 pint (1/2 cup) extra virgin olive oil
> 5 tablespoons wine vinegar
> 2 teaspoons salt
> water to dilute, about 500 ml/1 pint (2 cups)
> 1 bunch muscatel grapes, peeled and seeded

Soak the bread in water until softened. Grind the skinned almonds in a food processor with the garlic. Squeeze out the bread and add to the processor with just enough water to make a smooth paste. With the motor running, add the oil, then the vinegar and salt. Add a little of the water, then pour the mixture into a tureen or pitcher and add enough additional water to make the soup the consistency of cream. The soup should be quite tangy, so add additional vinegar if needed. Chill the soup. Stir before serving into bowls, each garnished with three or four grapes.

Serves 6.

STARTERS, SOUPS & SIDES

69

GREAT DISHES FROM SPAIN

STARTERS, SOUPS & SIDES

ESSENTIAL FLAVOUR: OLIVE OIL

It wouldn't be *gazpacho* without olive oil, which contributes flavour and creaminess to the blend. Nor would *paella* taste the same, nor fried fish, nor chicken in almond sauce. Olive oil is the most essential ingredient in Spanish cooking. Happily, modern medical research shows olive oil is good for you. It's probably the most healthful cooking fat of all, what makes the Mediterranean diet so alluring.

On the supermarket shelf you will find two categories of olive oil, one labelled simply, *aceite de oliva* — olive oil, and the other labelled *aceite de oliva virgen extra* — extra virgin olive oil. The first is actually refined olive oil, mild in flavour, without the fruitiness so prized in virgin oil. Virgin Extra is "olive juice", oil extracted solely by mechanical means, crushing and pressing, and not refined. It is considerably more expensive than refined oil.

Spain produces more olive oil than any other country in the world, and some of the best as well. About 75 per cent of it comes from Andalusia, particularly the provinces of Jaén and Córdoba. Each region favours certain olive varieties. For instance, in Andalusia, *picual*, *hojiblanca* and *picudo* are the main varieties, whereas Catalonia is known for its *arbequina* oil. While some producers feature a single varietal, it is more common to have blended oil. Some olive oil has *denominación de origen*, guaranteeing its quality and geographic origin.

Use extra virgin oil raw where you want the flavour to stand out — in salads, spooned over cooked fish, vegetables, baked potatoes and pasta. And, of course, in *gazpacho*. It's perfect for marinades, in sautés and braises, even for deep-frying.

Keep extra virgin olive oil in glass containers, in a cool place (not refrigerated) and, most importantly, protected from the light. Use it lavishly and enjoy wonderful flavour.

SEAFOOD CHOWDER WITH SHERRY
Gazpachuelo

Every stretch of coastline has a version of seafood soup. This one is typical of Málaga, where it's also known as *Sopa Viña AB*, named for a brand of sherry with which it is fortified. Make fish stock with heads, bones and trimmings from any white fish.

> 1200 ml/2 pints (5 cups) fish stock
> 1 large potato (280 g/10 ounces)
> 1 egg
> 125 ml/4 1/4 fl oz (1/2 cup) extra virgin olive oil
> 3 tablespoons lemon juice
> 280 g/10 ounces angler-fish (monkfish) fillets
> 40 g/1 1/2 oz *serrano* ham
> 2 tablespoons chopped *piquillo* pepper or red *pimiento*
> 6 tablespoons frozen peas
> 110 g/4 oz peeled prawns (shrimp)
> 2 tablespoons dry *fino* sherry

Place the fish stock in a soup pot and bring to a boil. Peel the potato and cut into small dice. Add to the broth, cover, and cook until potato is almost tender, about 10 minutes.

While potato is cooking, place the egg in a blender and blend 10 seconds. Gradually beat in the oil until emulsified. Blend in the lemon juice and reserve the mixture in the blender container.

Cut the anglerfish fillets into bite-size pieces. Dice the *serrano* ham. Chop the *piquillo* pepper.

When potatoes are almost tender, add the pieces of fish and peas to the soup. Simmer two to three minutes. Add the ham, *piquillo* pepper, and prawns. Let the soup come again to a gentle boil, two minutes. Add the sherry.

With the blender running, ladle hot broth into the reserved egg-oil mixture. Remove the soup from the heat and whisk the blender mixture into the soup.

Serve immediately in shallow soup bowls.

Serves 4.

STARTERS, SOUPS & SIDES

73

GREAT DISHES FROM SPAIN

CASTILIAN GARLIC SOUP
Sopa Castellana

Spain has garlic soup the way France has onion soup. Almost a cult, it is served in every region of the country. Wonderfully restorative. This version is typical of Madrid. It is frequently served in individual earthenware bowls, each with an egg poached in the hot soup, although you can simply poach the eggs right in the soup pan, then carefully ladle them into individual bowls. While usually served as a first course, with the egg added, it could be a simple supper dish.

> 6 tablespoons olive oil
> 6 cloves garlic, peeled and chopped
> 300 g/10 1/2 oz (10-12 slices) stale bread, cut in strips
> 1 tablespoon *pimentón* (paprika)
> pinch of cayenne (optional)
> 1 1/2 litres/3 pints (7 1/2 cups) chicken stock
> 2 teaspoons salt
> 6 eggs
> chopped parsley

In a soup pot heat the oil and fry the chopped garlic and strips of bread until lightly golden. Stir in the *pimentón* and cayenne, if using, then immediately add the stock and salt.

Bring the soup to a boil. Simmer until the bread is mostly dissolved, about 15 minutes. Ladle the boiling soup into individual ovenproof soup bowls and break an egg into each. Place them in a preheated hot oven until the whites are set but yolks still liquid. (Alternatively, poach eggs right in the soup pan.) Sprinkle each with a little chopped parsley.

Serves 6.

GARNISHED BROTH
Sopa de Picadillo

The broth which remains after serving *cocido*, an elaborate boiled dinner, is garnished with chopped ham and croutons to make a light evening meal. *Cocido* broth is very rich, with chicken, beef and ham boiled in it. The fresh mint sets off the aromas beautifully. If you haven't got real *cocido* broth, use any good chicken stock boiled with a piece of ham or unsmoked bacon.

Sopa de Picadillo is considered a hangover cure.

> 2 litres/4 pints (8 cups) chicken and ham broth
> 3 tablespoons olive oil
> 100 g/3 1/2 oz (3-4 slices) bread, diced
> 100 g/3 1/2 oz *serrano* ham, chopped
> 2 hard-boiled eggs, chopped
> 4 tablespoons dry sherry
> cooked chickpeas (*garbanzos*), optional
> sprigs of mint

If desired, skim the fat from the broth. Heat the broth.

In a frying pan heat the oil and fry the diced bread until golden. Remove and reserve. Immediately before serving add the ham, chopped egg, sherry and fried bread to the soup. Ladle the broth into soup plates and garnish each with a sprig of mint.

Serves 6.

STARTERS, SOUPS & SIDES

GREAT DISHES FROM SPAIN

STARTERS, SOUPS & SIDES

GALICIAN SOUP
Caldo Gallego

This *potaje* includes greens typical of Galicia, *grelos*, which are the stems and leaves of a sort of turnip. You could substitute chard, collards, spinach or cabbage for these turnip greens.

> 250 g/1/2 lb white cannellini beans, soaked overnight
> 3 litres/5 1/4 pints (3 quarts) water
> meaty ham bone, salt-cured pork ribs or a piece of fresh pork
> meaty beef marrowbone
> piece of salt pork fat
> 3 medium potatoes
> 1 kg/2 lbs greens, washed and chopped
> 1 teaspoon *pimentón* (paprika)
> salt

Drain the soaked beans and put them to cook in a large pot in water with the ham bone or pork, the beef bone and salt pork fat. When the beans are partially cooked, one hour, add the potatoes, peeled and cut in small chunks.

In a separate pot of boiling water, blanch the greens for three minutes. This removes excess bitterness. Add them to the beans and potatoes and taste for salt. Dissolve *pimentón* in a little of the soup and stir it in. Cook another 30 minutes until potatoes and greens are tender. To serve, cut meat off bones and discard bones.

Serves 8.

SIDE DISHES

SPINACH WITH RAISINS AND PINE NUTS
Espinacas con Pasas y Piñones

The best raisins of all are the sweet Málaga muscatel. However, you could use any type of raisin. Chard can be used in the recipe instead of the spinach.

> 1 1/2 kg/3 lbs spinach or chard, washed, trimmed and chopped
> 3 tablespoons olive oil
> 50 g/1 3/4 oz (1/3 cup) pine nuts
> 2 cloves garlic, chopped
> 80 g/3 oz (1/2 cup) raisins, seeded
> salt and pepper

In a large pan, heat the oil and fry the pine nuts just until they are golden. Skim them out and reserve. Add the chopped garlic and the spinach to the pan. Cook the spinach in the oil until wilted. Then add the raisins and salt and pepper and just a little water. Cover and cook the spinach 10 minutes. (Chard will need more cooking time, so add additional water.)

Stir the toasted pine nuts into the spinach and serve.

Serves 6 as a side dish.

STARTERS, SOUPS & SIDES

GREAT DISHES FROM SPAIN

STARTERS, SOUPS & SIDES

SUMMER VEGETABLE STEW
Pisto

Pisto, a mélange of aubergine (eggplant), courgette (zucchini), tomatoes and peppers, can be served cold as a starter or hot as a side dish. It makes a light meal topped with fried eggs.

> 680 g/1 1/2 lb aubergine (eggplant), about 2 medium, peeled and cut in 2 1/2 cm/1 inch cubes
> salt
> 3 tablespoons olive oil
> 1 onion, chopped
> 2 cloves garlic, chopped
> 1 green capsicum (bell) pepper, cut in 2 1/2 cm/1 inch squares
> 600 g/1 1/4 lb tomatoes, diced (3 cups)
> 450 g/1 lb courgette (zucchini), cut in 1-inch cubes
> 1 teaspoon salt
> 1 teaspoon crumbled dry oregano
> freshly ground black pepper
> 1/8 teaspoon cumin seeds
> chopped parsley

Place the cubed aubergine in a colander and sprinkle it liberally with salt. Let it drain for 1 hour.

In a casserole, heat the oil and sauté the onion and aubergine for five minutes. Add the garlic and green pepper and sauté another minute, then add the tomatoes and courgette. Sauté on a medium heat another five minutes.

Season with salt, oregano, pepper and cumin seeds. Cover and cook on a slow heat until vegetables are soft, about 20 minutes. It shouldn't be necessary to add additional liquid, but stir frequently so that the vegetables don't scorch.

Serve garnished with chopped parsley. If serving cold, a touch of vinegar is a good addition.

Serves 6.

BROAD BEANS WITH *SERRANO* HAM
Habas con Jamón

Tiny broad (fava) beans, in Spain called *habas baby*, are best because they cook quickly without the skins becoming tough.

This dish can be served as *tapa*, side dish, starter, or main course.

> 3 tablespoons olive oil
> 1 onion, chopped
> 1 clove chopped garlic
> 3 tablespoons chopped sweet red (bell) pepper
> 55 g/2 oz *serrano* ham, chopped
> 1400 g/3 lbs fresh broad (fava) beans, shelled (or 400 g/14 oz packet frozen)
> 1 teaspoon flour
> 250 ml/1/2 pint (1 cup) water
> 1/2 teaspoon salt
> freshly ground black pepper
> 1 tablespoon chopped parsley plus additional to serve

Heat the oil in a 20-cm/8-inch earthenware casserole or heavy enamelled casserole. Sauté the onion and garlic until softened, 5 minutes. Add the pepper and ham and sauté 2 minutes. Stir in the shelled beans and sauté 3 minutes. Sprinkle with the flour and stir.

Add water, salt, pepper and parsley. Bring to a boil, cover, and simmer until beans are tender, 15 to 20 minutes for small ones.

Sprinkle with additional chopped parsley to serve.

Serves 2 as a starter, 4 as a side.

STARTERS, SOUPS & SIDES

GREAT DISHES FROM SPAIN

SPANISH POTATO CASSEROLE
Cazuela de Patatas "A Lo Pobre"

The Spanish name, *a lo pobre*, means poor-man's-style, traditionally a main dish with no meat. This casserole makes a great side dish with meat or fish.

> 2 kg /4 lbs potatoes
> 2 onions
> 2 small sweet green peppers
> 1 tomato, sliced
> 150 ml/1/4 pint (2/3 cup) olive oil
> 3 cloves garlic, chopped
> 3 tablespoons chopped parsley
> 2 bay leaves
> 1/2 teaspoon thyme
> 1/2 teaspoon *pimentón* (paprika)
> 100 ml/3 1/2 fl oz (1/3 cup) white wine
> 100 ml/3 1/2 fl oz (1/3 cup) water
> salt and pepper

Peel the potatoes and slice them fairly thinly. Peel and slice the onions. Cut peppers in strips. Pour a little of the oil into the bottom of a flameproof earthenware casserole or oven-safe pan. Arrange alternating layers of potatoes, onions, green peppers and tomato slices, sprinkling each layer with some of the chopped garlic and parsley. Break the bay leaves into pieces and tuck them among the potatoes with the thyme. Sprinkle with the *pimentón* and pour over the remaining oil.

Place the casserole on a medium heat just until potatoes start to sizzle. Add the wine and water. Season with salt and pepper. When the liquid comes to a boil, cover the casserole with foil and put in a preheated medium oven (180ºC/350ºF) until potatoes are tender, about 45 minutes. Let the casserole rest 10 minutes before serving.

Serves 10 as a side dish.

FARM-STYLE FRIED BREAD CRUMBS
Migas a la Cortijera

Migas means "crumbs," crumbled stale bread fried up with bits of ham and garlic. On farmsteads, it is served as a hearty breakfast, sometimes accompanied by fried eggs. It also makes a fine side dish with pork chops.

The bread should be dense, fine-textured country bread, one to two days old.

> 225 g/8 oz stale bread (6-8 slices, to make 5 cups of diced bread)
> 125 ml/4 fl oz (1/2 cup) water
> 100 ml/3 1/2 fl oz (1/3 cup) olive oil
> 2 cloves garlic, quartered lengthwise
> 3 thick slices bacon (85 g/3 ounces), cut crosswise in strips
> 1/2 teaspoon salt
> 1 teaspoon *pimentón* (paprika)
> pinch of ground cumin
> pinch of ground cloves
> pinch of ground pepper
> a few grapes or raisins

Cut the bread into 1 1/4 cm/1/2 inch dice. Place the diced bread in a bowl and sprinkle with the water. Toss the bread bits until they are thoroughly dampened, but not soaked. Place them on a dampened kitchen towel and wrap them tightly. Leave to stand overnight (or at least six hours).

Heat the oil in a deep frying pan or earthenware casserole. Fry the pieces of garlic and strips of bacon until lightly browned, then skim them out and reserve.

Add the bread bits to the fat. Fry the crumbs on a medium heat, turning them constantly with a spatula. Keep stirring until they are loose and lightly toasted, about 20 minutes. Keep cutting the bread with the edge of the spatula to gradually reduce the dice into crumbs.

Stir in the salt, paprika, cumin, cloves and pepper. Return the fried garlic and bacon to the pan and give everything another few turns. Serve the crumbs hot, when they are slightly crunchy.

Serves 4 as a side dish.

STARTERS, SOUPS & SIDES

89

3
main dishes

Bubbling beans, savoury stews, glorious *paella*, stupendous fish, poultry and meat, even vegetarian — such are the choices for main dishes. Pick a salad or starter, add a sweet and accompany with a fine Spanish wine for a fantastic dining experience.

The recipes here are but a small sampling of the wonderful dishes in the Spanish repertory. Some others to try when you're visiting Spain: *fritura variada*, mixed fish fry, a specialty of the Costa del Sol; grilled red mullet; *suquet*, a Catalan seafood stew; *bacalao al pil pil*, a Basque dish of sizzling salt cod; roast chicken stuffed with sausage and fruits; braised rabbit with mountain herbs; meatballs in almond sauce; baby lamb or suckling pig roasted in a wood-fired oven, both typical of Segovia; pork fillet cooked with sherry; lamb stew, and *cocido*, a one-pot meal with chicken, beef, sausages, potatoes, chickpeas and vegetables.

91

GREAT DISHES FROM SPAIN

MAIN DISHES

ASTURIAN CASSEROLE OF BEANS AND SAUSAGES
Fabada Asturiana

Asturias is in the north of Spain on the Bay of Biscay, where winters can be very chilly. Beans bubbling in a clay pot are just the thing to ward off the cold and stick to the ribs. Asturian *fabes* are like plump dried lima or butter beans.

> 500 g/1 lb dried large white beans, soaked overnight in water
> 150 g/5 1/4 oz streaky bacon, in one piece
> 250 g/1/2 lb salt-cured pork hock or ham (if using dry, cured ham, soak it overnight)
> 250 g/1/2 lb *chorizo* sausage (preferably smoked Asturian)
> 250 g/1/2 lb black *morcilla* sausage (preferably smoked Asturian)
> 2 bay leaves
> 1/4 teaspoon saffron, crushed
> salt and pepper to taste

Drain the beans and put them in an earthenware casserole. Blanch the bacon in boiling water for three minutes and drain. Tuck the bacon into the beans and cover them with water. Bring to a boil and skim. Add the ham hock, *chorizo*, *morcilla* and bay leaves. Bring to a boil and skim again. Add saffron, dissolved in a little liquid. Then cover and cook very slowly, one to two hours, or until beans are very tender.

Add cold water during cooking so beans are always just barely covered with liquid. Taste for salt and pepper. Don't stir the beans, which breaks them up, but shake the casserole from time to time. Let the *fabada* rest for 15 minutes before serving.

Serves 6.

GREAT DISHES FROM SPAIN

MAIN DISHES

CHICKPEAS WITH SPINACH
Garbanzos con Espinacas

Here's a delightful vegetarian dish, typical of Sevilla where it's a popular *tapa*.

> 350 g/12 ounces washed and chopped spinach
> 3 tablespoons olive oil
> 1/2 onion, chopped
> 1 tomato, peeled, seeded, and chopped
> 2 (570g/20 oz) jars chickpeas (5 cups)
> 1/8 teaspoon saffron threads
> 2 cloves garlic, coarsely chopped
> 1/2 teaspoon coarse salt
> freshly ground black pepper
> 2 teaspoons sweet *pimentón* (paprika)
> 1/4 teaspoon ground cumin
> pinch of ground cloves
> 120 ml/4 fl oz (1/2 cup) water

Place the spinach in a pot with a little water. Bring to a boil and cook until spinach is wilted. Drain and reserve.

Heat the oil in a deep frying pan or earthenware *cazuela*. Sauté the onion until softened, three minutes. Add the tomatoes and sauté two minutes.

Crush the saffron in a mortar. Add the garlic and salt and grind the garlic to a paste. (This can also be done in a blender.) Add the pepper, paprika, cumin and cloves. Stir the water into the paste. Add the mortar mixture to the frying pan (skillet). Add the chickpeas without draining. Add the spinach. Bring to a boil then reduce heat.

Cover the pan and let the chickpeas simmer 15 minutes.

Serve in soup bowls. Serves 4.

LENTIL POT
Potaje de Lentejas

The spicy taste of *morcilla*, blood sausage, adds to this dish. If blood sausage is hard to find, use any pork sausage and add an extra pinch of cloves, pepper, *pimentón* and cinnamon. You could use either the tiny dark brown lentils or the larger green ones.

- 450 g/1 lb lentils
- 2 litres/3 1/4 pints (8 cups) water
- 3 tablespoons olive oil
- 1 tomato, peeled and chopped
- 1 sweet green (bell) pepper, cut in pieces
- 1 onion, quartered
- 3 carrots, peeled and sliced
- 2 bay leaves
- 1 head garlic, roasted (directions below)
- 1 tablespoon salt
- 2 cloves
- 2 large potatoes, chopped
- 1 teaspoon *pimentón* (paprika)
- 1/2 teaspoon ground cumin
- 1/4 teaspoon ground black pepper
- dash of cayenne
- 350 g/12 oz *chorizo* sausage links (or any pork sausage)
- 115 g/4 oz *morcilla* (black) sausage (optional)
- 2 tablespoons sherry vinegar or wine vinegar

Combine the lentils and water in a large pot. Bring to a boil and skim. Add the oil, tomato, green pepper, onion, carrots, bay leaves and cloves of roasted garlic to the lentils with the salt. Bring to a boil and simmer for 20 minutes.

Add the potatoes, *pimentón*, cumin, pepper and cayenne. Add the sausages and cook the lentils until everything is tender, another 30 minutes. Before serving, add the vinegar.

Serves 6.

To roast a whole head of garlic: Spear the head of garlic on a fork or grasp it with tongs and hold over a gas flame or put under the grill (broiler), turning, until it is charred. Peel the garlic cloves, rinse in running water and add them to the stew.

MAIN DISHES

GREAT DISHES FROM SPAIN

PAELLA WITH SEAFOOD
Paella Con Mariscos

Authentic Valencia *paella* contains no seafood at all. It's made with chicken or rabbit, snails and two kinds of beans. But this version, with shellfish and chicken, is very popular throughout the country. A typical *paella* pan, often used on a wood fire out of doors, is wide and flat and quite unwieldy on the kitchen hob (stove). You might try using a deeper pan — a flat-bottomed wok works well — or your largest frying pan.

MAIN DISHES

Spanish rice is a medium-short grain variety, not long-grained pilaff style rice. It soaks up the delicious flavours with which it cooks, but gets sticky if overcooked. If Spanish rice isn't on your supermarket shelf, look for Italian *arborio* rice, the sort used for *risotto*.

If you don't have real saffron, use a spoonful of *pimentón* (paprika) for authentic flavour plus a few drops of yellow food colouring to get that wonderful sunny yellow colour. (No, don't use that other yellow spice, turmeric, because it has a strong, sharp flavour of its own, which doesn't jibe with Spanish flavours.)

A stock made with chicken carcass plus prawn (shrimp) shells will add to the *paella*'s flavour.

1 dozen mussels, scrubbed and steamed open
500 g/1 lb large, uncooked *langostinos* (prawns or jumbo shrimp)
6 tablespoons olive oil
1 kg/2 lbs chicken or rabbit, cut in small pieces
300 g/10 oz squid, cleaned and cut in rings
1 green sweet (bell) pepper, cut in squares
2 large tomatoes, peeled and chopped
2 cloves garlic, minced
100 g/3 1/2 oz shelled peas or broad (fava) beans, green beans or quartered artichokes (parboil beans or artichokes)
1 1/2 litres/2 1/2 pints (6 1/2 cups) water or stock
500 g/1 lb (2 1/2 cups) Spanish medium-short grain rice
1/2 teaspoon saffron (or more, for a bright yellow colour)
sprig of fresh rosemary
freshly ground black pepper
2 teaspoons salt
1 tinned red *pimiento*, cut in strips
lemon for garnish

Discard the empty half-shells of the mussels. Strain the liquid and reserve it. Cook 6-8 unpeeled prawns (shrimp) in boiling water for one minute. Set them aside and add the liquid to the mussel liquid. Shell the remaining uncooked prawns.

Heat the oil in a *paella* pan or large frying pan (approximately 40 cm/16 inch). Fry the chicken pieces in the oil very slowly until browned. Add the squid. Continue frying, adding next the green peppers, then the tomato, garlic and peas, beans or artichokes. Combine the reserved mussel liquid and stock or water to make 1 1/2 litres/2 1/2 pints (6 1/2 cups). Add all but one cupful of the liquid to the *paella*.

Crush the saffron in a mortar or in a teacup using the butt end of a knife. Dissolve it in a little water or white wine and stir into the *paella* with the rosemary, pepper and salt. Add the peeled prawns.

When the liquid comes to a boil, add the rice and continue to cook on a high heat for six to eight minutes. Reduce the heat and continue to cook until rice is just barely tender, adding the additional liquid as needed, about ten minutes more. Don't stir the rice, but shake the pan. Garnish the top with the reserved mussels, cooked prawns and strips of *pimiento*. Let the *paella* rest for five minutes before serving with lemon wedges.

Serves 6.

THE SPICES OF LIFE

Such a tantalizing palette of colours and aromas at the spice vendors' stalls! It's enough to inspire you to get cooking.

Few dishes in Spanish cuisine could be described as "spicy". The use of spices and herbs in Spanish cookery is subtle but essential, giving distinctive flavour to many dishes — saffron to colour and aromatise rice dishes; nutmeg in meatballs; thyme in rabbit stew; a sprig of fresh mint in consommé.

Saffron, which is grown in the central region of La Mancha, consists of deep red filaments, the stigmas of an autumn-blooming crocus. It takes approximately 70,000 flowers to produce 450 g/1 lb of spice. Crushed and infused in warm liquid, saffron threads add that glorious golden colour to cooked foods, essential for *paella*, as well as a mildly bitter floral taste. Truth be told, not all paellas served up to tourists at restaurants on Spanish coasts are made with real saffron. Many get their brilliant yellow from inexpensive artificial colouring.

Purchase saffron in *hebras*, threads, and store it tightly covered in a cool, dry, dark place. Should a friend bring you a prized souvenir from Spain, a "jewel box" of golden saffron, enjoy it within a year.

One gram, about 1/10 of one ounce, is a sufficient quantity for about six recipes for *paella*, risotto, or chicken in saffron-almond sauce.

To extract the full flavour and colour from saffron, first crush it in a small mortar. Perfectly dry saffron will pulverise easily. If you don't have a mortar and pestle, use the butt end of a knife to crush the saffron in a teacup. Add enough liquid — wine or hot water, milk, or broth — to cover the crushed saffron. Let it infuse at least 10 minutes and up to 45 minutes. Stir the crushed saffron and its liquid into rice or sauce.

The most widely used spice in Spanish cooking is *pimentón* or paprika. *Pimentón*, made from dried and finely ground red peppers, comes sweet (*dulce*), bittersweet (*agridulce*) and spicy-hot (*picante*), depending on the variety of pepper. In Murcia in eastern Spain *pimentón* peppers are sun-dried, but in Extremadura, where fall weather can be wet, they are smoke-dried over smouldering wild oak, giving the *pimentón* an earthy, toasty flavour.

Smoked *pimentón* carries the label "Pimentón de la Vera", the place where it is produced. Considered a gourmet product, it's not easy to find at ordinary spice markets.

Use sweet *pimentón* by heaping spoonfuls to add taste to almost any stew. Smoked *pimentón* is especially good in marinades and in barbecue sauces, but it can overpower delicate foods such as fish.

Other spices much used in Spanish cookery are aniseed, which goes into Christmas sweets; cinnamon, clove, cumin, chilli, pepper, nutmeg and sesame seed. The most favoured herbs are parsley, first and foremost, with bay leaf, mint, oregano, rosemary and thyme. Pots of sweet basil are sold at garden shops, but the herb is rarely used in Spanish cooking.

Purchase spices and herbs from open stock at market stalls. Store them tightly capped and protected from light. Most lose their pungency and aroma in a year, so replace them as needed.

PASTA *PAELLA* WITH SEAFOOD
Fideuá

If you think pasta belongs only to the Italians and noodles to the Asians, think again. In Spain, pasta talks Spanish (or Catalan) and the word is *fideos (fideus* in Catalan). *Fideos* are thin, round noodles or tiny elbows with a pinhole through the middle. In Valencia *fideos* stand in for rice in a tasty *paella*. The pasta is cooked right in the pan or casserole, with only enough liquid to keep it juicy.

Use solid-fleshed fish cut either in thick crosswise steaks or in fillets. Good choices are angler-fish (monkfish), grouper, snapper or one of the "rockfish," such as scorpion fish, weever or gurnard. Use heads and trimmings to make a flavourful stock.

For the *sofrito* and fish:
3 tablespoons olive oil
400 g/14 oz (2 cups) chopped tomatoes
100 g/3 1/2 oz (1/2 cup) chopped green sweet pepper
3 cloves chopped garlic
1 tablespoon *pimentón* (paprika)
2 teaspoons salt
2 litres/3 1/4 pints (8 cups) water
1 small squid (280g/10 ounces), cut in squares
1250-1360 g/2 1/2 to 3 lb whole fish, cut in thick steaks or fillets

For the pasta:
3 tablespoons olive oil
230 g/1/2 lb small *langostinos* or *cigalas* (see note below)
450 g/1 lb pasta (elbow *fideos* or spaghetti broken into short lengths)
hot fish stock with squid and *sofrito* (above)
1/4 teaspoon saffron threads, crushed
1/4 teaspoon ground cumin
freshly ground pepper
115 g/4 oz peeled prawns (shrimp)
sprigs of fresh mint to garnish
alioli garlic sauce to serve with the fish (recipe follows)

Note: confusion can arise over the names in Spanish, French and English for prawns and lobsters. *Langostinos* are king prawns or

MAIN DISHES

jumbo shrimps. *Cigalas* are known to the British as *scampi*, Dublin Bay prawns, or Norway lobster, to the Americans as sea crayfish and to the French as *langoustines*.

Heat the oil in a soup pot and fry the tomatoes, pepper and garlic until softened, five minutes. Stir in the *pimentón*. Add the salt, cut-up squid, and water. Any fish heads can be added too. Bring to a boil and simmer, covered, 20 minutes. Remove and discard fish heads.

Bring again to a boil and add the fish steaks or fillets. Cook at a simmer until the fish flakes when probed with a skewer, about

12 minutes. With a skimmer, remove the fish to a platter.

In a casserole or 35 cm/14 inch *paella* pan heat the oil and sauté the unpeeled *langostinos* or *cigalas*, turning to cook on both sides, for about four minutes. Remove and set aside.

Add the pasta to the pan and toast it in the oil, stirring constantly, until lightly golden. Add 1180 ml/2 pints (5 cups) of the hot fish stock with the pieces of squid and bring to a boil. Dissolve the crushed saffron, cumin and pepper in 120 ml/4 fl oz (1/2 cup) of the liquid and stir it into the pasta. Taste for salt, adding more if necessary.

Cook the pasta on a hot fire for five minutes. Stir in the peeled prawns. Arrange the cooked fish and sautéed *cigalas* on top of the pasta. Cook another two minutes or until pasta is tender. The pasta should be juicy, but not soupy. Allow the pasta to rest five minutes before serving. Garnish with mint sprigs. Serve accompanied by the *alioli*.

Serves 4-6.

GARLIC MAYONNAISE
Alioli

Serve this pungent sauce with grilled fish, barbecue, chips (fries), vegetables, as well as with rice dishes.

> 2 cloves garlic
> 1 egg, at room temperature
> 175 ml/6 fl oz (3/4 cup) extra virgin olive oil
> 1 teaspoon salt
> 2 tablespoons fresh lemon juice or vinegar

Put the garlic and egg in a blender and pulse until garlic is finely chopped. With the motor running, pour in the oil in a slow trickle, allowing it to be absorbed by the egg before adding more. Blend in all the oil until the sauce is emulsified and thickened. Add the salt and lemon juice.

MAIN DISHES

BASQUE - STYLE HAKE
Merluza a la Vasca

Hake is a delicate fish, related to cod. This Basque-style preparation is sometimes called "hake in green sauce." Green with lots of chopped parsley.

> 1 1/2 kg/3 lbs fresh hake steaks or fillets
> salt
> 2 tablespoons flour
> 100 ml/3 1/2 fl oz (1/3 cup) olive oil
> 6 cloves garlic, sliced crosswise
> 150 ml/1/4 pint (2/3 cup) white wine
> 1/2 teaspoon salt
> 50 g/2 oz peas
> 150 g/5 oz clams
> a few peeled prawns (shrimp), if desired
> 2 tablespoons chopped parsley
> 6 cooked or tinned asparagus spears

Salt the fresh fish steaks and let them stand for 15 minutes. Then pat dry and dust them with flour. Heat the oil in a flameproof earthenware casserole or frying pan. Add the sliced garlic and the pieces of hake. Let them cook, without browning, for two minutes on each side.

Add the wine, salt, peas, clams and, if desired, a few prawns. Cook the fish, shaking and rocking the casserole, until the fish is just flaky and clamshells opened. The sauce should be slightly thickened. Add the chopped parsley and asparagus.

Serves 6.

MAIN DISHES

GREAT DISHES FROM SPAIN

MAIN DISHES

BAKED FISH WITH POTATOES
Pescado al Horno

This dish is typical of beach restaurants along the Málaga and Cádiz coasts. Use a large whole sea bream (*besugo*) or sea bass (*lubina*). A whole fish weighing 2 kg/4-5 lb will serve 6 people.

> 1 whole sea bream, weighing about 2 kg/4-5 lb, gutted and scaled
> salt
> 5 tablespoons olive oil
> 1 kg/2 lb baking potatoes, peeled and sliced thinly
> 5 cloves garlic, chopped
> 3 tablespoons chopped parsley
> 1 green sweet pepper, chopped
> salt and pepper
> 1 onion, sliced
> 2 tomatoes, sliced
> 2 bay leaves, broken into pieces
> 120 ml/4 fl oz (1/2 cup) dry white wine

Rub fresh fish inside and out with salt and leave it to set for 30 minutes. Rinse and pat dry.

Pour half the oil into a flameproof oven pan large enough to hold the fish. Add half the sliced potatoes. Scatter with half the garlic, parsley and peppers. Sprinkle with salt and pepper. Add all the sliced onions, most of the tomatoes, then the remaining potatoes, garlic, parsley and peppers. Sprinkle with salt and pepper.

Place the fish on top of the potatoes and arrange the remaining slices of tomato on top. Drizzle with remaining oil. Tuck in the pieces of bay leaf. Pour the wine over and put on a medium heat until the liquid begins to simmer. Then cover the pan with foil and bake in a preheated medium (180ºC/ 350ºF) oven until the potatoes are tender, 45 minutes. Remove the foil and bake 10 minutes longer.

Serves 6.

109

BREAM, GRILLED ON ITS BACK
Besugo a la Espalda

Is this the greatest of Spanish seafood dishes? So simple, so delicious. *Besugo* is red bream, but any large sea bream (porgy or sheepshead), sea bass or snapper could be prepared this way. Smaller fish, one per serving, can be prepared in the same manner. Cook the fish over charcoal or under a grill (broiler).

Have the fish gutted but not scaled and split open along the belly and butterflied. Leave the backbone in. Open the fish out flat, salt it lightly and let it rest 30 minutes at room temperature.

- 1 whole sea bream, weighing about 900 g/2 lb (with or without head)
- salt
- 2 1/2 tablespoons olive oil
- 1 teaspoon coarse salt
- 2 cloves garlic, sliced crosswise
- red pepper flakes, tiny chillies or sliced rings of dried red chili (to taste)
- 1 teaspoon vinegar
- 1 teaspoon water

Coat a grill (broiler) pan with oil and sprinkle with coarse salt. Preheat the pan under the grill (broiler).

Pat the fish dry with paper towels. Brush skin and flesh sides with half a tablespoon of olive oil. Lay the fish, skin-side down, on the heated pan and grill (broil) 10 cm/ 4 inches from the heat. When the fish is cooked, you should be able to lift out the spine and discard it. This will take about 10 minutes. Don't turn the fish.

While the fish is cooking, in a small pan place two tablespoons of oil, sliced garlic and red pepper flakes. Heat until the oil begins to sizzle and garlic begins to turn golden, less than one minute. Remove from heat and immediately add the vinegar and water.

Transfer the grilled fish to a heated platter and serve it, on its back, with the garlic oil spooned over it.

Serves 2.

MAIN DISHES

CHICKEN SIZZLED WITH GARLIC
Pollo al Ajillo

Aficionados of this dish insist on lots of garlic, but disagree as to whether the garlic should be peeled, chopped and fried, or whether whole cloves of garlic should cook with the chicken. While the *tapa* bar version usually consists of chicken hacked into small bits, this interpretation of the classic calls for chicken wing joints, which cook quickly, but avoid nasty bone splinters. If you're cooking it as a main course dish, use a jointed chicken, but allow longer cooking time and more liquid. Incidentally, this dish is also made with rabbit.

> 1 dozen chicken wings, jointed, and wing tips discarded
> 6 tablespoons olive oil
> 10 cloves garlic
> 1 bay leaf
> 150 ml/1/4 pint (2/3 cup) dry or medium-dry sherry
> salt and pepper
> chopped parsley

Lightly smash the garlic cloves to split the skins. Set aside five of them, unpeeled. Peel the remaining cloves and slice them. Heat the oil in a deep frying pan. Add the sliced garlic and sauté just until golden, then skim it out and reserve.

Add the chicken pieces to the oil and fry them slowly, adding the unpeeled cloves of garlic. When chicken is browned, add the bay leaf, sherry, salt and pepper. Continue cooking until liquid is nearly absorbed and the chicken begins to sizzle again. Serve immediately garnished with chopped parsley and the reserved sautéed garlic bits.

Makes 24 pieces.

MAIN DISHES

CHICKEN IN ALMOND SAUCE
Pollo en Pepitoria

Almond trees blossom pale pink in late winter. The nuts, which are harvested in the early fall, are widely used in Spanish cooking. Almonds are the main ingredient in *turrón*, nougat candy, and marzipan, both popular at Christmas time. They also go into many savoury dishes such as this chicken fricassee. Steamed rice is a good side dish with the chicken.

> 1 large chicken or boiling fowl (2-3 kg/4 1/2 to 6 1/2 lb), jointed
> salt and pepper
> flour
> 5 tablespoons olive oil
> 40 g/1 1/2 oz (1/3 cup) almonds, blanched and skinned
> 6 cloves garlic, peeled
> 50 g/2 oz (2 slices) bread, crusts removed
> 1 onion, chopped
> 1 clove
> 10 peppercorns
> 1/2 teaspoon saffron
> 1 teaspoon salt
> 1 tablespoon chopped parsley
> 140 ml/1/2 pint (2/3 cup) dry sherry or white wine
> 250 ml/8 fl oz (1 cup) chicken stock
> 1 bay leaf
> 2 hard-boiled egg yolks
> 1 tablespoon slivered almonds, fried in a little oil until golden
> triangles of fried bread

Rub the chicken pieces with salt and pepper and dredge them with flour. Heat the oil in a frying pan and fry the almonds, four cloves of garlic and the bread slices until they are golden and skim out. In the same oil, brown the chicken pieces very slowly on both sides, adding the chopped onion. Remove the chicken to a flameproof casserole.

In a mortar, grind the clove, peppercorns and saffron with the salt. Add the fried garlic, the remaining two cloves of raw garlic, almonds and bread (this can be done in a blender or processor), then the parsley. Dilute this mixture with some of the wine and stir it into the chicken pieces. Add the remaining wine and stock. Bring to a boil and simmer, covered, very gently until the chicken is tender (1-2 hours, depending on size of the chicken).

Mash the egg yolks with a little of the liquid and stir it into the casserole to thicken the sauce. Serve the chicken garnished with the toasted slivered almonds and triangles of fried bread. Serves 6.

MAIN DISHES

GREAT DISHES FROM SPAIN

MAIN DISHES

HERB-MARINATED PORK LOIN
Lomo en Adobo

You'll find this tasty pork loin served as a *tapa*, when it is thinly sliced and quickly fried, then served atop a piece of bread, called a *montadito* or *planchita*. In this version, the whole loin is oven-roasted, then sliced. It makes a nice dish for a buffet supper.

> 1 1/2 kg/3 lbs boned pork loin
> 4 cloves garlic, crushed
> 1 teaspoon *pimentón* (paprika)
> 2 teaspoons oregano
> pinch of thyme
> pinch of rosemary
> 10 peppercorns
> 1 teaspoon salt
> 1 tablespoon olive oil
> 180 ml/6 fl oz (3/4 cup) wine vinegar (preferably sherry vinegar)

Combine the crushed garlic, *pimentón*, oregano, thyme and rosemary. Rub the pork loin with this mixture. Place the loin in a non-reactive container. Sprinkle with the peppercorns, salt and oil. Pour over the vinegar. Cover the container and marinate the pork, refrigerated, for two days. Turn the pork in the marinade twice a day.

Drain the meat and pat it dry and place in a roasting pan. Put it in a hot oven (200ºC/400ºF) for 10 minutes to brown. Then reduce the heat to medium (180ºC/350ºF) and roast until the pork is done. Test it after one hour — cut into the centre of the piece of meat. Meat should be juicy, only slightly pink in the centre. If still red, roast another 15-20 minutes. Allow the meat to rest for 10 minutes before slicing. Serve hot or cold.

Makes 8 main course servings.

GREAT DISHES FROM SPAIN

MAIN DISHES

LAMB BRAISED WITH SWEET PEPPERS
Cordero al Chilindrón

This dish is from Aragón, a region that grows wonderfully sweet peppers. The usual interpretation is lamb cut in chunks as for stew. In this version, tender little lamb chops are used. This is a good way to cook chicken, too.

> 1 kg/2 lbs lamb chops, trimmed of excess fat
> salt and pepper
> 4 sweet red (bell) peppers
> 3 tablespoons olive oil
> 3 cloves garlic, chopped
> 150 g/5 oz *serrano* ham, cut in strips
> 1 small onion, chopped
> 3 large tomatoes, peeled and chopped

Rub the chops with salt and pepper. Roast the peppers under the grill (broiler) or over a gas flame, turning until they are blistered and charred. Remove and let them rest, covered. Then peel them and cut the flesh into wide strips.

Heat the oil in a flameproof casserole and brown the lamb chops on both sides. Remove the chops.

Add the chopped garlic, strips of ham, chopped onion and strips of pepper. Add the chopped tomatoes and cook briskly for 10 minutes until tomatoes are somewhat reduced.

Return the lamb to the pan. Reduce heat and simmer until lamb is cooked through, about 12 minutes.

Serves 4.

GREAT DISHES FROM SPAIN

MAIN DISHES

BULL'S TAIL (BRAISED OX-TAIL)
Rabo de Toro

The bullfighter whose art is most highly rated in the *plaza de toros* is awarded trophies for his performance: one ear, two ears, and the tail too for the most profound *faena*. You won't have to brave any fighting bulls to enjoy this dish, for butchers' oxtail works just fine. This slow-simmered dish produces a deep, rich gravy, good with potatoes or rice on the side.

> 1 whole oxtail, cut crosswise into 8 cm/3 inch pieces
> 3 tablespoons olive oil
> 1 onion, chopped
> 1 leek, chopped
> 3 carrots, diced
> 2 cloves garlic, chopped
> 50 g/2 oz *serrano* ham or bacon, chopped
> 5 tablespoons brandy
> 120 ml/4 fl oz (1/2 cup) dry sherry or red wine
> 1 tomato, peeled and chopped
> 1 bay leaf
> sprig of parsley
> sprig of thyme
> salt and freshly ground black pepper
> pinch of ground cloves
> chopped parsley

Blanch the pieces of oxtail in boiling water for five minutes and drain. In a large pan or casserole, heat the oil and add the onion, leek, carrots, garlic and ham and sauté until onion is softened. Add the pieces of oxtail and brown them on a high heat. Add the brandy, set it alight, and stir until the flames subside. Then add the sherry or red wine, chopped tomato, herbs, salt and pepper and cloves.

Simmer until the meat is very tender, about two hours, adding additional liquid as needed. The sauce should be fairly thick. If necessary, thicken with a little flour whisked into the gravy. If desired, this dish can be prepared in advance, chilled, and excess fat skimmed off. This also allows flavours to mellow. Serve garnished with chopped parsley.

Serves 4.

BRAISED PARTRIDGE, TOLEDO STYLE
Perdiz Estofada a la Toledana

Spain is known as the partridge capital of Europe. During the autumn shooting season you may find this handsome bird on sale at meat markets. This manner of preparing partridge, braised with lots of onions, is traditional in the Montes de Toledo, the mountainous region in the south part of Toledo province. If partridge is not available, try the dish with Cornish game hen or plump little poussin.

> 4 partridges, small chickens, or Cornish game hens (each about 450 g/1 lb)
> salt
> freshly ground black pepper
> sprigs rosemary
> 120 ml/4 fl oz (1/4 cup) olive oil
> 2 onions, halved and sliced
> 1 carrot, diced
> 30 g/1 oz *serrano* ham or bacon, diced (1/4 cup)
> 6 cloves garlic, chopped
> 2 tablespoons chopped parsley
> 1/2 teaspoon dried thyme
> 2 bay leaves
> 350 ml/12 fl oz (1 1/2 cups) white wine

Sprinkle the birds inside and out with salt and pepper. Tuck a small sprig of rosemary in the cavity of each. Tie the birds with kitchen string to keep legs and wings close to the bodies. Allow them to stand 30 minutes at room temperature.

Heat the oil in a deep sauté pan or casserole. Brown the partridges on all sides on medium to high heat, 10 minutes. Remove them.

Add the onions and carrot to the remaining oil. Sauté on medium-high heat until onions begin to brown, 10 minutes. Add the ham or bacon and garlic. Place the partridge on top of the onions. Sprinkle with the parsley and thyme. Tuck the bay leaves between the birds. Pour over the wine. Bring to a boil, cover. Reduce heat so the liquid just simmers.

Cook the partridge 20 minutes, then turn them and cook,

covered, until they are very tender, 35 to 45 minutes longer.

Remove partridge to a platter. Cook remaining onions and liquid, uncovered, until slightly reduced. Remove strings from partridge. Serve with the onion sauce.

Serves 4.

4
pastries & puddings

Spain has such a fabulous repertoire of pastries, cakes, puddings and *dulcería* (sweet things) that it's a tough call to select just a few of the most representative. Every village has its favourites. For every saint's day celebration, Easter and the 12 days of Christmas, beloved pastries and desserts sweeten the occasion.

Fabulous fresh fruit is a favourite dessert in Spain, for which no recipes need be given. Just look for the best of seasonal fruit: summer — peaches, plums, melon, figs, grapes; autumn — apples, pears, persimmons, pomegranates, quinces; winter — oranges, avocados, custard apples (*chirimoya*), clementines; and spring — strawberries, apricots and loquats (*níspero*).

Puddings and custards include: *flan*, or caramel custard, a real treat when homemade; *natillas*, a creamy custard; rice pudding dusted with cinnamon; *crema catalana*, the Catalan version of *crème brûlée*, and *tocino del cielo*, a very dense custard, so rich it is cut into tiny squares. Cakes, pies, pastries, biscuits (cookies), confections and candies are likely to grace that hallowed afternoon snack, *merienda*, which happens around 6 pm. Browse a *pastelería*, pastry shop to select your favourites.

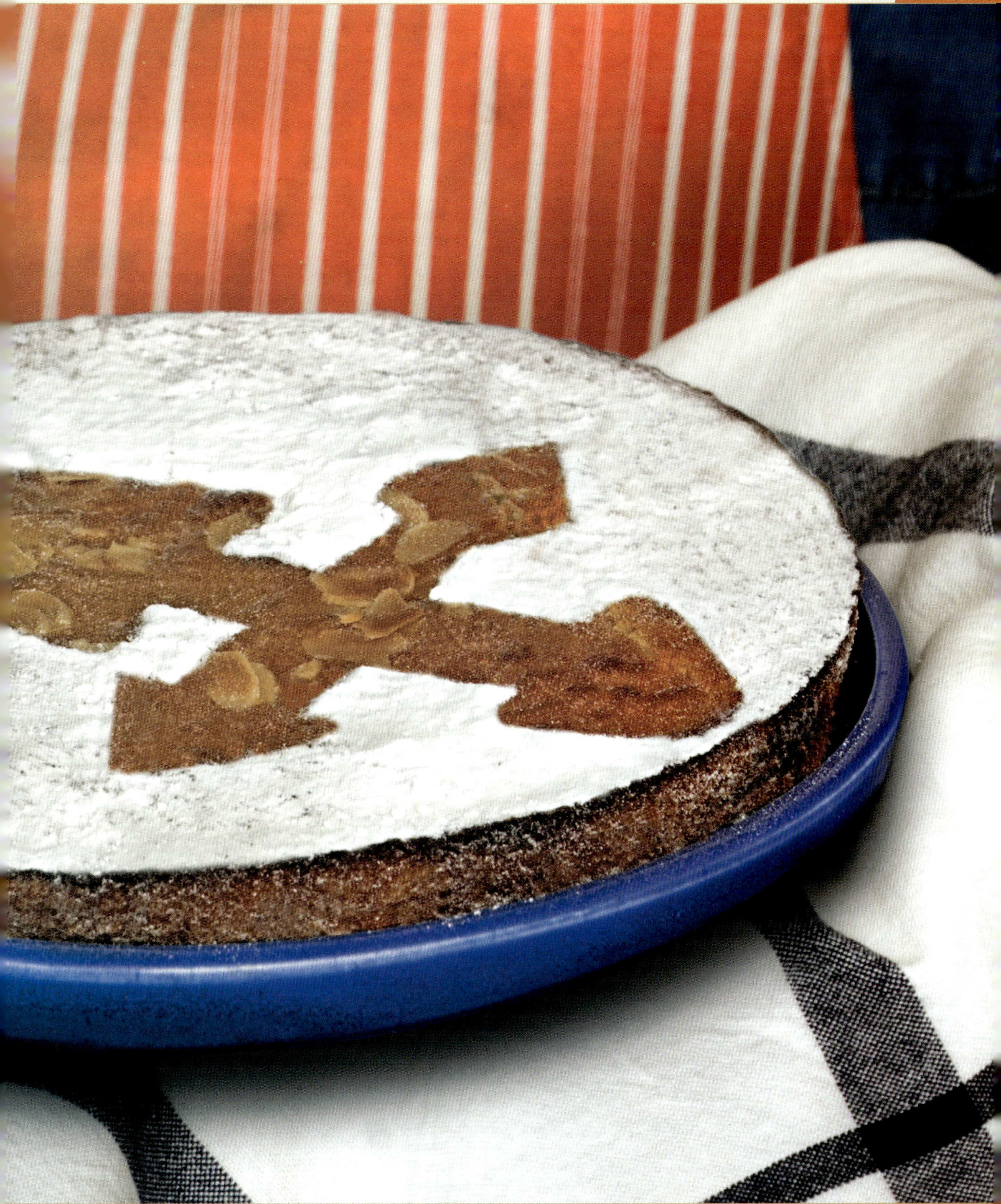

CATALAN CUSTARD WITH BURNT SUGAR TOPPING
Crema Catalana

A salamander is not a mythical beast, but a kitchen tool for caramelising a sugar topping. Consisting of an iron disk on a rod, it is heated red-hot and laid on sugar until it browns and melts. Nowadays there are electric salamanders. Or use a small kitchen blowtorch.

> 6 egg yolks
> 150 g/5 1/4 oz (3/4 cup) sugar
> 750 ml/1 pint 6 fl oz (3 1/4 cups) milk
> zest of 1 lemon
> 6 cm/2 inch cinnamon stick
> 100 ml/3 1/2 fl oz (1/3 cup + 1 tablespoon) milk
> 3 tablespoons cornflour (cornstarch)
> 50 g/1 3/4 oz (1/4 cup) sugar

In a bowl beat the egg yolks with the 150 g/5 1/4 oz sugar. Put the 750 ml/1 pint 6 fl oz milk in a pan with the lemon zest and cinnamon stick. Bring to a boil and remove from heat. Strain it and whisk into the beaten yolks. Stir the remaining milk and cornflour together in a small bowl until smooth. Stir it into the custard mixture. Cook the custard on a low heat, stirring constantly, until it just begins to bubble. Remove from the heat and divide between six shallow pudding dishes. Cool the custard.

Shortly before serving, sprinkle the tops of the custards with the remaining sugar. Use a salamander, heated on a gas flame, to caramelize the top of each custard.

Serves 6.

PASTRIES & PUDDINGS

CREAMY RICE PUDDING WITH CINNAMON
Arroz Con Leche

Rather better than the nursery pudding you remember. It's a favourite dessert amongst Spain's yuppies and politicians, perhaps for the comfort value. Make a more sophisticated version by sprinkling the top with sugar and caramelising it as in the previous recipe.

> 200 g/7 oz (1 cup) short-grain (pudding) rice
> 250 ml/9 fl oz (1 cup) water
> 1 piece cinnamon stick
> strip of lemon zest
> 100 g/3 1/2 oz (1/2 cup) sugar
> pinch of salt
> 1 1/4 litres/2 pints (5 1/4 cups) milk
> additional sugar
> ground cinnamon

Put the rice and water to cook in a saucepan. Bring to a boil, cover and simmer just until the water is absorbed, about six minutes. Add the cinnamon stick, lemon zest, sugar, salt and milk. Bring to a boil, then turn the heat to very low and cook, covered, until the rice is tender, another 20 minutes.

Remove the cinnamon stick and lemon peel. While the pudding is still hot, spoon it into a serving bowl or individual pudding dishes. Sprinkle with additional sugar and dust thickly with cinnamon. Cool. The pudding should still be creamy, not set too firm.

Makes 6-8 servings.

PASTRIES & PUDDINGS

SANTIAGO ALMOND TORTE
Torta de Santiago

This torte comes from Santiago de Compostela in northern Spain, where the shrine of St. James (Santiago) is located. Usually the torte has the outline of the cross of St. James on its top, but it's just as delicious without the symbol.

> 450 g/1 lb almonds, blanched, skinned and finely ground
> 150 g/5 1/4 oz (2/3 cup) butter
> 500 g/1 lb 2 oz (2 3/4 cups) sugar
> 7 eggs
> 150 g/5 1/4 oz (1 1/4 cups) plain flour
> 1 tablespoon grated lemon zest
> icing (confectioners') sugar

Spread the ground almonds in an oven tin and toast them in a preheated moderate oven, stirring frequently, until they are lightly golden. Take care they do not brown. Cool.

Cream the butter and sugar until light and fluffy. Beat in the eggs one at a time, then stir in the flour, ground almonds and grated lemon zest. Pour into a buttered springform tin (pan) and bake in a preheated moderate oven (180° C/350°F) until a skewer inserted in the centre comes out clean, about one hour. Cool the torte 10 minutes, then remove from the tin and cool on a rack.

Before serving dust the top with icing sugar. If desired, place a template of the Santiago pilgrim's cross on the torte, sprinkle with sugar, brush sugar off the template and remove it.

Serves 10, cut in thin wedges. This torte is good served with fruit purées.

PASTRIES & PUDDINGS

GREAT DISHES FROM SPAIN

PASTRIES & PUDDINGS

SWEET FRITTERS
Buñuelos

These puffed fritters, fried in oil, are made by street vendors and are especially enjoyed on fiesta days, often accompanied by thick, hot chocolate. They're best freshly made.

> 240 ml/8 1/2 fl oz (1 cup) milk or water
> 70 g/2 1/2 oz (1/3 cup) butter
> 30 g/1 oz (2 tablespoons) sugar
> pinch of salt
> 125 g/4 1/2 oz (1 cup) plain flour
> 3 eggs, room temperature
> olive oil for deep frying the fritters
> sugar

Place the milk or water, butter, sugar and salt in a saucepan and bring to a boil. Add the flour all at once, beating it hard with a wooden spoon. As you continue beating, it will form a smooth ball of dough. Remove from the heat and beat in the eggs, one at a time, until each is incorporated. Continue beating the batter until cool. (Batter can be prepared in advance.)

Heat the oil in a deep fryer or heavy frying pan. Drop the batter into the hot oil by spoonfuls. The batter will puff as it fries. Turn the fritters to brown both sides. Remove, drain and sprinkle the fritters with sugar.

Makes about 24 fritters.

GREAT DISHES FROM SPAIN

ANISE-FLAVOURED HOLIDAY RINGS
Roscos de Navidad

Spain's version of the doughnut, scented with anise and cinnamon, is one of the favourite sweets at Christmas time. Typically, in regions that produce huge quantities of olive oil, they would be fried in this oil. You can substitute other vegetable oil.

> 200 ml/7 fl oz (3/4 cup + 1 tablespoon) olive oil
> 3 tablespoons aniseeds
> zest of a small lemon, removed in one piece
> 180 g/6 1/3 oz (1 cup) sugar
> 200 ml/7 fl oz (3/4 cup + 1 tablespoon) white wine
> 2 teaspoons cinnamon
> 1 kg/2 lbs 3 oz (7 1/2 cups) plain flour
> 2 eggs, separated
> 3 teaspoons bicarbonate of soda (baking soda)
> oil for deep-frying
> 140 g/5 oz (2/3 cup) sugar

Place the 200 ml/7 fl oz of oil in a frying pan and heat it with the piece of lemon peel. Add the aniseeds and cook a few minutes just until the spice is fragrant. Remove and cool the oil. Skim out and discard the lemon zest.

In a bowl, combine the 180 g/6 1/3 oz of sugar with the wine, cinnamon and oil. Add 260 g/9 oz (2 cups) of the flour. Beat in the egg yolks and bicarbonate of soda.

Beat the egg whites until stiff and fold them into the batter. Gradually add the remaining flour, using the hands to work it in. The dough will be very sticky. Continue adding flour until it forms a soft dough that doesn't stick to the fingers. Take a small ball of the dough and roll it into a cord about 10 cm/4 in long. Pinch the ends together to form a circle. Continue forming the rings.

Heat oil in a deep fryer or deep frying pan until hot but not smoking and fry the rings, a few at a time, until golden on both sides. Remove them with a skimmer, drain briefly, and, while still hot, dredge them in the remaining sugar.

Makes 6-7 dozen small rings.

MERINGUE MILK ICE
Leche Merengada

This is a specialty at *heladerías*, ice cream shops, especially popular in the Valencia region.

> 1 litre/2 pints (4 cups) milk
> 200 g/7 oz (1 cup) sugar
> zest from 2 lemons
> 4 cm/2 inch cinnamon stick
> 1 clove
> 3 egg whites
> 1/2 teaspoon lemon juice
> 1 teaspoon ground cinnamon

Put the milk, sugar, lemon zest, cinnamon stick and clove in a pan. Simmer, stirring frequently, for 10 minutes. Strain the milk into a metal bowl. Chill the milk.

Place the milk in the freezer until it is soft-frozen. Stir it occasionally to mix the frozen and liquid milk.

Beat the egg whites on high speed until they hold stiff peaks. Beat in the lemon juice.

Beat the soft-frozen milk at high speed until smooth. On low speed, beat in half of the egg whites. Fold in remaining egg whites by hand, mixing thoroughly.

Serve the ice meringue milk immediately or return it to the freezer to freeze slightly longer. It should be the consistency of soft-freeze ice cream. If allowed to hard-freeze, remove it from the freezer about 40 minutes before serving, so it begins to thaw.

Serve the milk ice in tall glasses or goblets and sprinkle each serving with cinnamon.

Serves 6.

PASTRIES & PUDDINGS

HOLIDAY SWEETS AND NATURAL DELIGHTS

As the Christmas season nears, several aisles in Spanish supermarkets are taken over by counters laden with sweetmeats for the holidays. Boxed assortments contain *mantecados*, a crumbly, lard biscuit (cookie) with cinnamon and sesame seed; *polvorones*, delicate biscuits dusted with icing sugar, and *roscos de vino*, tiny rings with sweet wine and cinnamon.

Essential for these festive occasions is *turrón*, almond nougat candy. Most famous is that from Jijona (Alicante). It even has its own protected denomination. Turrón comes in two styles: hard, with whole almonds in a honey-nougat, and soft, of a fudgy consistency.

Also made with Spanish almonds is *mazapán* (marzipan) a dense, sweet almond paste that for Christmas is moulded into fanciful shapes. Toledo's marzipan is world-famous.

For the Twelfth night of Christmas, the feast of the Three Kings, you place an order at a bake shop for a *roscón de reyes*, a ring cake studded with dried fruits and usually filled with whipped cream. It has a little trinket baked in it. The one who finds it is guaranteed a sweet year.

Especially beloved at Christmastime are pastries fried in olive oil. Look for these at bakeries and in small neighbourhood shops, where they are usually made by the proprietor or her neighbours. These include *empanadi-*

PASTRIES & PUDDINGS

llas, little fried pies with a filling of sweet potato or pumpkin jam, *pestiños*, sesame-studded fried twists, and *roscos*, fried doughnuts with anise flavour.

While almond-based sweets and anise-spiked pastries point to a Moorish heritage, those with chocolate date from Spain's colonisation of the New World, where the wondrous chocolate bean was discovered. For a century Spain had virtually a monopoly on the importation and distribution of chocolate. Barcelona, known for its confectionery, produces figures of sculpted chocolate as gift items at Easter.

Be sure to sample thick, hot drinking chocolate that's more like pudding than cocoa. Dunk fried *churros* into it for breakfast or at the end of a night of partying. At the store, you can purchase *chocolate a la taza*, bars of chocolate already sweetened and thickened for whisking with hot water or milk to make drinking chocolate.

From Extremadura comes a delightful gift item, chocolate-covered figs (look for them in gourmet sections of El Corte Inglés department stores).

Also confected from dried figs is *pan de higos*, a fig roll or round spiced with cinnamon, clove, sesame and anise and studded with almonds. Slice it and serve on a sweets tray.

Quince, a fruit that looks like a knobbly, oversized apple, also makes an appearance in the repertoire of sweets. Rich in pectin, the pureed fruit is cooked with sugar to make quince jelly or quince paste, *dulce de membrillo*, that sets up solid enough to cut in slices. Serve it with breakfast toast, on a cheese board, or paired with salty Manchego cheese as an aperitif.

Fruit jams and conserves, especially marmalade from bitter Seville oranges, are other gastronomic choices. Look for single-flower honeys too. Especially appreciated are orange-blossom honey from Valencia and rosemary honey from Guadalajara.

Every town market has a stall specialising in *frutos secos* (dried fruits). Apart from dried figs, apricots, and dates, they also offer every sort of nut. Almonds are the star (unskinned, blanched, fried, slivered, ground), but look for hazelnuts, walnuts, pine nuts, chestnuts, peanuts and tiger nuts as well. This last item, tiger nuts, *chufas*, which are actually tubers, not nuts, are used to make a delightful sweet drink called *horchata*, a specialty of Valencia. You can buy it bottled, but it's especially good made fresh or frozen at an ice cream shop.

You will surely discover your own favourite sweets and pastries, many of which are purely local. But don't neglect the packaged pastries to be found in any supermarket. Some to look for: *ensaimadas*, Mallorcan spiral buns, really good for breakfast; *tortas de aceite* crisp, flat olive oil pastries, good with tea or with sweet sherry; *magdalenas*, small sponge cakes, for dipping into coffee.

GLOSSARY

Spanish Ingredients and Utensils

Anchovies (*boquerones, anchoas*). Fresh anchovies are small silvery fish — very different from salty, tinned ones — which can be prepared in many ways. If not available, substitute strips of fresh sardines, herring or mackerel.

Casserole (*cazuela*). Earthenware casseroles with unglazed bottoms can be used for cooking on a gas hob (stove top) or in the oven. If not available, use any flameproof casserole or frying pan. Earthenware holds the heat after it has been removed from heat, so food continues to cook.

Chorizo. Spain's most distinctive sausage. It is coloured red with paprika and flavoured with garlic. There are two types of *chorizo*: a hard-cured sausage, which is sliced and served as cold cuts, and a soft sausage, usually tied in links, which can be fried or added to *potajes* (thick soups).

Cod, dry salt codfish (*bacalao*). A favourite ingredient everywhere in Spain. Salt cod must be soaked for 24 to 36 hours in several changes of water before being prepared. (An exception is the recipe in this book for salad with oranges, where the cod is merely toasted.)

Denomination of origin (*denominación de origen*; DO). Used for wines as well as many foods, such as olive oil, cheese and ham, to designate geographic origin and guarantee of production and quality. It is the Spanish equivalent of the French *appelation d'origine contrôlée*.

Ham (*jamón*). In Spain ham usually means *serrano* ham. This is a salt-cured ham (not smoked), which is served raw, very thinly sliced, as a *tapa* or aperitif. It is also used in cooked dishes. *Prosciutto* or Parma ham is the closest substitute, though unsmoked gammon or back bacon could be used in cooked dishes. Ordinary cooked ham, the sort you might use for a ham sandwich, is *jamón cocido*. (More about ham on page 24)

Morcilla. A black sausage made from pig's blood and seasoned with cinnamon, cloves, nutmeg, fennel, sometimes pine nuts or onions. It is stewed with pulses and vegetables in typical stews or thick soups.

Mortar and pestle (*almirez, mortero*). A mortar of brass (*almirez*), marble or wood is useful for crushing saffron threads or whole spices such as peppercorns and cloves.

Olive oil (*aceite de oliva*). An essential flavour in Spanish cooking. The finest is

GLOSSARY

virgen extra, **extra virgin**, oil extracted by purely mechanical means. The other type, simply labelled *aceite de oliva*, **olive oil**, is oil that has been refined then mixed with some virgin oil to restore the olive oil flavour. (More about olive oil on page 71.)

Paella. This rice dish is named for the utensil in which it is cooked, a wide, flat pan which allows all the ingredients to cook in a single layer over a fast-burning fire or, nowadays, on a large gas ring. A *paella* pan large enough to serve eight people (40 cm/15-16 in) is hard to manage on a hob, though you can try placing it over two burners. It's easier to make two *paellas* or use a deeper pan. The pans are sold in hardware stores and supermarkets all over Spain. They are usually made of rolled steel, which rusts. After use, scour the pan and dry very thoroughly before storing. If you wish to keep leftover *paella*, store it refrigerated in a covered container and reheat in a microwave.

Peppers, capsicums, paprika. Spanish markets offer a number of different sorts of capsicum peppers: huge bell peppers (*pimientos*) in green, red and yellow; crinkly, skinny green ones with a crisp taste; small piquant-sweet red *piquillo* peppers, which are usually peeled and canned; tiny green Padrón peppers for frying; dried sweet, red peppers, such as *ñoras* and *choriceros*, which are used to flavour *chorizo* sausage. Several sorts of chilli peppers can be found too, most fairly mild. Chilli is not widely used in Spanish cooking. *Pimentón* (paprika), a spice made by grinding dried red peppers, can be sweet or piquant. (More about *pimentón* on page 101.)

Rice (*arroz*). Use medium-short grain rice, not pilaff rice, for Spanish rice dishes such as *paella*. It does not need washing before cooking. Spanish rice needs careful monitoring while it cooks as, overcooked, it can be sticky. Remove from heat source when it is still slightly *al dente* (taste it) and allow to rest five minutes to finish cooking from residual heat. Actual cooking time varies considerably, depending on what type of pan and quantities of liquid used. So, for example, rice in a *paella* pan cooks more quickly than in an earthenware *cazuela*.

Saffron (*azafrán*). This costly spice is grown in Spain. The spice, wispy threads of a deep orange colour, should be crushed (with a mortar and pestle, or in a teacup with the butt-end of a knife), then dissolved in a little liquid before adding to the food to be cooked. If real saffron is not available, use instead a spoonful of paprika and/or a few drops of yellow food colouring.

Vinegar (*vinagre*). Wine vinegar is used in Spanish cooking. There are some special ones — red wine vinegar from Rioja, sherry vinegar from Jerez, and *cava* vinegar from Catalonia.

Wine (*vino*). Wine used in Spanish cooking is usually white table wine (*blanco*); dry sherry (*vino fino de Jerez*), or medium sherry (*vino oloroso* or *amontillado de Jerez*. (For more about wines to serve with meals, see page 42.)

INDEX

ajo blanco con uvas, 68
alioli, 104
almejas a la marinera, 64
almond sauce, chicken in, 114
almond torte, Santiago, 130
anchovies, marinated fresh, 18
Andalusian tomato soup, cold, 67
anise-flavoured holiday rings, 135
arroz con leche, 128
Asturian casserole of beans and sausages, 93

baked eggs, flamenco style, 57
baked fish with potatoes, 109
Basque-style hake, 106
beans and sausages, Asturian casserole of, 93
beans with serrano ham, broad, 84
besugo a la espalda, 110
boquerones al natural, 18
braised lamb with sweet peppers, 119
braised partridge, Toledo style, 122
bread crumbs, farm-style fried, 88
bream, grilled on its back, 110
broad beans with serrano ham, 84
broth, garnished, 76
bull's tail (braised ox-tail), 121
buñuelos, 133

caldo gallego, 79
Canary Islands wrinkly potatoes with spicy herb sauces, 26
casserole of beans and sausages, Asturian, 93
casserole, Spanish potato, 87
Castilian garlic soup, 75
Catalan custard with burnt sugar topping, 126
Catalan tomato toasts, 22
cazón en adobo, 30
cazuela de patatas "a lo pobre", 87
cheese, 34
chicken in almond sauce, 114
chicken sizzled with garlic, 112
chickpeas with spinach, 95
chilli sauce, green, 26

chilli sauce, red, 27
chorizo, 25
chowder with Sherry, seafood, 72
clams, fishermen's style, 64
cocktail, shellfish, 14
cod salad, orange and, 48
cold Andalusian tomato soup, 67
cold white garlic soup with grapes, 68
cordero al chilindrón, 119
creamy rice pudding with cinnamon, 128
crema catalana, 126
custard, Catalan with burnt sugar topping, 126

eggs scrambled with mushrooms, prawns and green garlic, 54
eggs, flamenco style, baked, 57
empanada gallega, 50
ensalada de pimientos asados, 20
espinacas con pasas y piñones, 80

fabada asturiana, 93
farm-style fried bread crumbs, 88
fideuá, 102
fish, marinated fried, 30
fish, peppers stuffed with, 58
fish with potatoes, baked, 109
fishermen's style, clams, 64
flamenco style, baked eggs, 57
fried bread crumbs, farm-style, 88
fried fish, marinated, 30
fritters, sweet, 133

Galician pork pie, 50
Galician soup, 79
Galician-style, octopus, 62
gambas al ajillo, 40
gambas en gabardinas, 33
garbanzos con espinacas, 95
garlic, chicken sizzled with, 112
garlic mayonnaise, 104
garlic soup with grapes, cold white, 68
garlic soup, Castilian, 75
garlic, eggs scrambled with mushrooms, prawns and green, 54

INDEX

garlic-sizzled prawns, 40
garnished broth, 76
gazpacho andaluz, 67
gazpachuelo, 72
green chilli sauce, 26
grilled prawns with romesco sauce, 61

habas con jamón, 84
hake, Basque-style, 106
ham, 24
ham, broad beans with serrano, 84
herb-marinated pork loin, 117
holiday rings, anise-flavoured, 135
hot potatoes, 29
how to slice serrano ham, 24
huevos a la flamenca, 57
huevos revueltos con setas, gambas y ajetes, 54

ibérico ham, 24

kebabs, spicy pork, 39

lamb braised with sweet peppers, 119
langostinos a la plancha con salsa de romesco, 61
leche merengada, 136
lentil pot, 96
lomo en adobo, 117

marinated fresh anchovies, 18
marinated fried fish, 30
mayonnaise, garlic, 104
mejillones a la vinagreta, 17
meringue milk ice, 136
merluza a la vasca, 106
migas a la cortijera, 88
milk ice, meringue, 136
mojo colorado, 27
mojo verde, 26
mushrooms, prawns and green garlic, eggs scrambled with, 54
mussels vinaigrette, 17

octopus, Galician-style, 62
olive oil, 71
olives, 53
omelette, Spanish potato, 36
orange and cod salad, 48
ox-tail, braised (bull's tail), 121

paella con mariscos, 98
paella with seafood, 98
paella, pasta with seafood, 102
pan amb tomat, 22
papas arrugadas con mojo, 26
partridge, braised, Toledo style, 122
pasta paella with seafood, 102
pastries, about, 138
patatas "a lo pobre", 87
patatas bravas, 29
pepper salad, roasted, 20
peppers stuffed with fish, 58
perdiz estofada a la toledana, 122
pescado al horno, 109
pie, Galician pork, 50
pimentón, 101
pimientos de piquillo rellenos con pescado, 58
pinchitos morunos, 39
pisto, 83
pollo al ajillo, 112
pollo en pepitoria, 114
pork kebabs, spicy, 39
pork loin, herb-marinated, 117
pork pie, Galician, 50
potaje de lentejas, 96
potato casserole, Spanish, 87
potato omelette, Spanish, 36
potatoes with spicy herb sauces, Canary Islands wrinkly, 26
potatoes, baked fish with, 109
potatoes, hot, 29
prawns and green garlic, eggs scrambled with mushrooms, 54
prawns in raincoats, 33
prawns with romesco sauce, grilled, 61
prawns, garlic-sizzled, 40
pudding, creamy rice with cinnamon, 128
pulpo a la gallega, 62

rabo de toro, 121
raisins and pine nuts, spinach with, 80
red chilli sauce, 27
red wine fruit punch, 44
remojón, 48
rice pudding with cinnamon, creamy, 128
rings, anise-flavoured holiday, 135
roasted pepper salad, 20
romesco sauce, grilled prawns with, 61
roscos de Navidad, 135

saffron, 101
salad, orange and cod, 48
salad, roasted pepper, 20
salpicón de mariscos, 14
sangría, 44
Santiago almond torte, 130
sauce, green chilli, 26
sauce, grilled prawns with romesco, 61
sauce, red chilli, 27
sausages, beans and, Asturian casserole of, 93
scrambled with mushrooms, prawns and green garlic, eggs, 54
seafood chowder with Sherry, 72
seafood, paella with, 98
seafood, pasta paella with, 102
serrano ham, 24
shellfish cocktail, 14
Sherry, 42
sopa castellana, 75
sopa de picadillo, 76
soup with grapes, cold white garlic, 68
soup, Castilian garlic, 75
soup, cold Andalusian tomato, 67
soup, Galician, 79
Spanish potato casserole, 87

Spanish potato omelette, 36
spices, 101
spicy herb sauces, Canary Islands wrinkly potatoes with, 26
spicy pork kebabs, 39
spinach with raisins and pine nuts, 80
spinach, chickpeas with, 95
stew, summer vegetable, 83
summer vegetable stew, 83
sweet fritters, 133

tapas, about, 12
toasts, Catalan tomato, 22
tomato soup, cold Andalusian, 67
tomato toasts, Catalan, 22
torta de Santiago, 130
torte, Santiago almond, 130
tortilla española, 36

vegetable stew, summer, 83
vinaigrette, mussels, 17

white garlic soup with grapes, cold, 68
wine, 42
wine fruit punch, red, 44
wrinkly potatoes with spicy herb sauces, Canary Islands, 26